INCLUDES
DVD
VIDEO

REFINISHING FURNITURE

MADE SIMPLE

JEFF JEWITT

The Taunton Press

To my wife Susan, whose enthusiasm and patience always help to bring my books to life.

The Taunton Press

The Taunton Press, Inc., 63 South Main Street, PO Box 5506, Newtown, CT 06470-5506
e-mail: tp@taunton.com

Editor: Castle Hill Media LLC
Copy editor: Candace B. Levy
Indexer: Jay Kreider
Interior design: Susan Fazekas
Layout: Castle Hill Media LLC
Photographer: Gary Junken except front cover, p. 2-5, 6 (top), 7, 8 (top and center left), 10-13, 14 (both top and center), 15–18, 20–24, 25 (top and center), 26, 27 (both top), 28-36, 40, 42 (bottom), 43 (both right), 48–50, 64, 66 (left), 69 (bottom), 71 (bottom right), 76, 78 (bottom), 79 (bottom), 80 (bottom), 81 (bottom), 82 (both top), 83 (bottom), 85, 93 (bottom right), 94, 107 (right), 110, 112 (bottom right), 113, 114 (top) © Susan Lawson Jewitt
DVD Production: Onsite Productions
DVD Editing: The Dream Tree

Library of Congress Cataloging-in-Publication Data

Jewitt, Jeff.
  Refinishing furniture made simple / Jeff Jewitt.
    p. cm.
  ISBN 978-1-60085-390-6
1. Furniture finishing. 2. Furniture--Repairing. I. Title.
  TT325.J422 2012
  684.1'043--dc23
                    2012018411

Printed in the United States of America
10 9 8 7 6 5 4 3 2 1

Working wood is inherently dangerous. Using hand or power tools improperly or ignoring safety practices can lead to permanent injury or even death. Don't try to perform operations you learn about here (or elsewhere) unless you're certain they are safe for you. If something about an operation doesn't feel right, don't do it. Look for another way. We want you to enjoy the craft, so please keep safety foremost in your mind whenever you're in the shop.

acknowledgments

I'd like to thank the following individuals and companies who helped out in the production of this book and video.

At Castle Hill Media, Helen Albert, who prodded me into starting this project and who wore many hats. At the Taunton Press, Gary Junken, who is the master behind the DVD videography and editing. Also, Peter Chapman, Jessica DiDonato, Katy Binder, and Carolyn Mandarano. Thanks to you all.

I'd also like to thank Tom Monahan at General Finishes, who provided time, advice, and waterborne finishing products. Also, Vince Valentino at Cleveland Lumber

Finally, my wife, Susan, who always helps on photography and keeps my writing concise and things flowing while I'm working on books and videos.

contents

Evaluating your project

W ood furniture and finishes deteriorate over time. Air, sun, humidity, and heat all contribute to this process. There also may be damage caused by hard use or just plain neglect.

Most people have a piece of furniture in their homes that could use some cosmetic repair: furniture with white rings from glasses or stray marks from crayons and felt-tip pens, an inherited antique with sentimental value, or a grimy but otherwise "perfect" piece from a garage sale. All can benefit from some cleaning, touchup, or refinishing.

Probably the most important question you need to answer before tackling any project is whether it is worth the time and effort? To make the decision, you'll need to evaluate what steps you must take to achieve the result you intend. Different interventions require more or less time and effort. But sometimes a big effort won't necessarily give a much better result. The only way to decide is to do an evaluation.

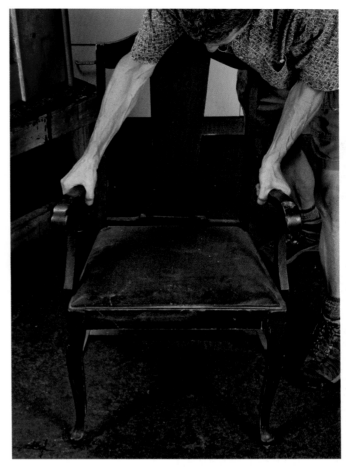

If you wiggle a chair, you should be able to flex it only slightly if it's in good shape. Joints that need repair will pop open or show part of the bare wood at the joint.

The five-point exam

Some problems are obvious, such as missing parts, like drawers, or badly damaged tops. Other problems require a little more detective work. This first exam will help you decide whether you may want to pass on a potential project due to the need for excessive or complicated repairs.

1. Place the item firmly on a level surface, grasp it by the sides or top, and gently wiggle it back and forth. This will telegraph any loose joints that will need to be reglued before any refinishing work can begin. Go over the item carefully noting anything unusual, such as screws, nails, or pieces of wood holding joints together. As long as there are no broken joints or other big problems, a simple regluing isn't hard to do.

It's common to find poorly done repairs lurking in unseen places. The glue holding the ledge on the base of this table failed. A strip of wood was nailed beneath it to hold the base together.

A missing glue block is one of the more common structural repairs, but fixing it doesn't require a lot of skill.

2. Look for large cracks and splits, missing hardware, or moldings. These are difficult repairs and require woodworking skills and specialized tools. Turn the piece over and look for the condition of the base, feet, or casters and unseen problems such as water damage and mold. Also look for missing glue blocks, which are small pieces of wood used to reinforce legs and other parts that need strength. (Glue blocks are easy to make and replace.)

3. Examine the overall condition of the finish. Is it a color you like and one that fits in with your decorating plan? Is it intact? Is wood visible underneath? Is the finish consistent and lacking large areas of discoloration? If the answer is yes on all counts, you may need only to clean and revive the finish rather than stripping it. If not, plan on stripping the finish. In the case of dark water stains, you may also need to follow special bleaching procedures to remove them. Some dark finishes may not lighten enough when you strip them, so don't plan on a light finish for dark-finished items.

This coat rack has a very dark dye stain under the finish that I have started to remove. Don't expect a light appearance when you strip something like this.

Wiping an old finish with paint thinner will reveal problems that can be corrected only by stripping, sanding, and refinishing.

4. Pull open drawers and doors and check for problems such as sticking doors, loose hinges, and poorly operating drawers. If the drawer sides are significantly worn, you may need to rebuild them—a task that requires good woodworking skills and tools.

5. Finally check for prior repairs that may have not been done correctly, such as joints that won't fit together because of failed attempts to reglue the parts. Fixing this problem requires dismantling the joint completely and cleaning and scraping away the old glue.

This first exam will reveal any structural problems that may be beyond your woodworking skills. In that case, you may want to pass on refinishing the piece unless you find a professional to do the work. If the piece passes this first exam, you can then move on to evaluating the finish.

This drawer has about ½ in. of wood worn from the bottom, which makes the drawer sloppy and hard to operate. Fixing this requires intermediate woodworking skills.

Water-damaged furniture

Water damage is the most common problem you'll encounter. It can be as minor as black rings from glasses or something more complicated, such as warped and split wood. Older furniture may have spent time in a garage or basement, so the first thing to do is to look underneath for evidence of mold or dampness. Check the wood at the bottom for rotted parts or wood that's worn away. Making new parts for furniture requires woodworking skills and tools. Severely water-damaged finishes will appear chalky or white or simply flake off. As long as the wood underneath is sound, stripping is the way to go for these items.

In the case of black rings or blotchy dark areas, as on this oak chest, you'll have to strip the finish, then bleach the black marks.

workSmart

Both for evaluation and for cleaning away heavy grime from most furniture, mineral spirits can't be beat. It will also reveal blemishes, such as scratches and gouges in bare wood.

Evaluating finishes

Once you've determined that the project piece is basically sound or that you can repair it easily, you can move on to evaluating the finish.

Clear finishes

To see if a finish is intact and may need only to be cleaned or revived (see Chapter 4), wipe the surface with a rag dampened with mineral spirits. If the solvent-dampened surface looks even and the grain of the wood is visible, chances are you can clean or revive the existing finish. Check underneath for mold and mildew, which can be removed with a 50:50 mix of water and chlorine bleach. If the solvent-dampened surface looks uneven or you see large discolored white or black-gray areas, then the piece has been water damaged and stripping is usually required.

Paint

Painted items are always a great deal at flea markets and antiques stores and may look like good projects, but always be wary of paint. In addition to the difficulty of

Kits for testing painted finishes for lead are available at paint stores and home centers.

If flaking paint reveals shiny areas, it was applied over a clear finish and thus should be fairly easy to strip.

stripping the piece, old paint may contain lead, which poses some safety issues. You can check for lead paints with simple-to-use kits available at paint stores and home centers (see "Testing for lead paint," on p. 9). The reason the furniture was painted also plays into the decision to work on the piece:

• *Paint was applied to make the furniture fit in with a decorating scheme.* This is the best-case scenario for painted furniture that you want to strip because the paint was simply applied over the existing finish. The paint should strip off fairly easily because the stripper will work under the existing original clear finish. Rub a coin or a key on a painted surface to see if there's finish under the flaked-off paint. If so, you can try stripping a small section such as a door or some molding to see if the paint comes off easily.

• *Paint was used to cover up problems* like large areas of wood that were damaged (cigarette or candle burns). Or perhaps putty or some other type of nonwood product was used to fill deep scratches, gouges, or missing wood.

• *Paint was the original finish.* Not only will it be hard to remove from the wood and grain but there may also be different species of wood used in construction and it will never look right with a clear finish. If there are a lot of complicated grooves and details, the paint may be especially difficult to remove.

Valuable antiques

As a general rule, if you suspect that an item is valuable, you should consult a pro. If that's not an option, then I suggest you do only simple repairs like regluing, cleaning the finish, and applying wax. If the finish doesn't perk up to your liking, you could remove the finish and apply a new one. However, stripping and refinishing antiques usually lowers their resale and historic value.

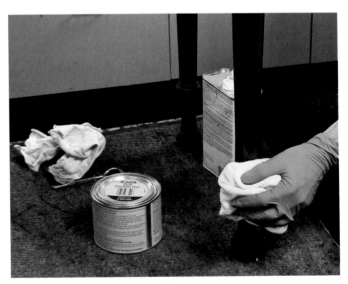

On valuable antique furniture the best strategy is to do a light cleaning followed by waxing.

The mineral-spirits-wipe test

This old desk and pine nightstand looked dirty and needed to be cleaned, but I also wanted to make sure that there were no problems lurking underneath the finish. A quick wipe down with paint thinner told me what I needed to do.

1. **Wipe the project's top with** paint thinner (or mineral spirits). Wetting the surface with solvent will reveal black areas caused by water (as seen under the rag).

2. **Wipe all vertical surfaces** with solvent to reveal any areas of missing finish.

3. **Use solvent to show crazing** (large cracks in the finish), such as on these stretchers.

4. **Wet surfaces after cleaning** to see scratches and gouges. Although the only damage that appeared on the pine top before wiping with solvent was the white ring, the solvent-wetted surface shows large scratches and gouges in the wood (darker brown areas).

Testing for lead paint

You can purchase lead paint test kits at most home centers and paint stores. Although most kits work more or less the same, carefully read the instructions that come with your kit.

1. **Press hard on the test vial** at the points indicated. This allows the two chemicals inside to mix.

2. **Squeeze the tube** (shaking it briefly beforehand helps) until you see a drop of colored liquid at the applicator head.

3. **Rub the applicator** on a small test area of the paint in question.

4. **Check the applicator color** after several seconds. The presence of lead paint will turn it a red color. Note the color chart card at top left in the photo. Most kits will have something comparable. Use it to compare the color if you aren't sure.

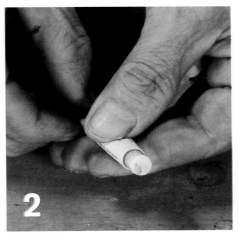

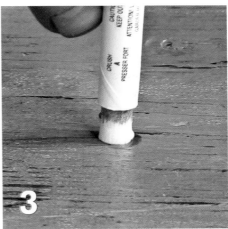

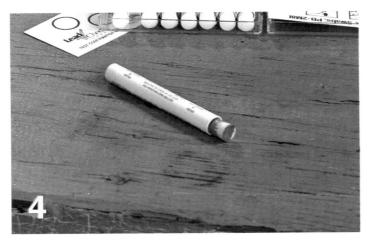

Why I should have passed on this Victorian chest

This little Victorian chest looks like a promising project, and the dealer was asking only $90.00. Unfortunately, I was in a hurry and didn't check it out as carefully as I should have.

A. Where some of the paint had come off at the base, I could see nice wood. Overall, the piece was really heavy, indicating all solid wood construction.

B. My first test used the back of a brass key to rub off some paint. I rubbed as hard as I could, but the paint wasn't budging. This is often a sign that paint was applied to the bare wood.

C. The insides of the drawers and the cabinet as well as the back and bottom were also painted.

D. The top drawer was really stuck. It may work better after all the paint is off, but you'll never know until you actually strip it.

E. At the antiques store, I missed the structural repair at the base. Gluing this correctly involves taking off the top as well as the side in question.

F. All these grooves and details will make stripping the paint difficult and time-consuming. Plus an examination of the back revealed that the underlying wood was oak. Getting all the paint out of an open-grained wood like oak will be tedious, if not impossible. I decided to pass on this project.

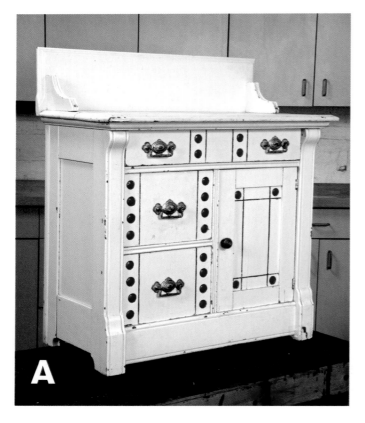

A

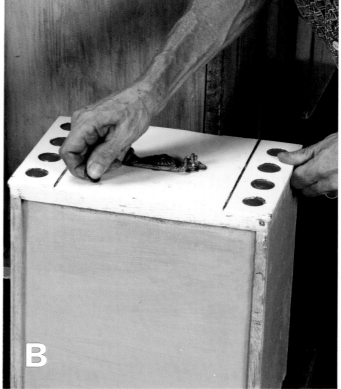

B

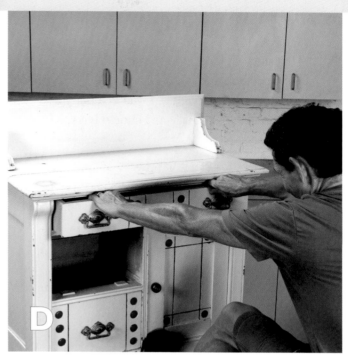

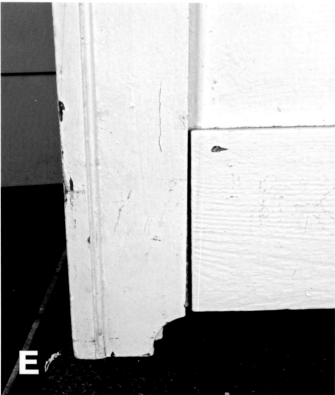

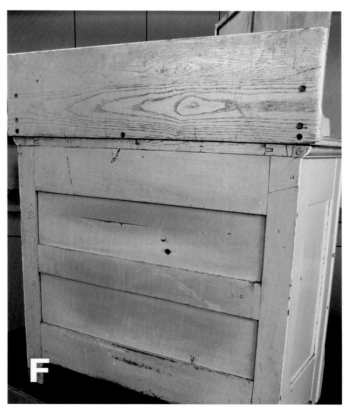

Tools and
solvents

Most refinishing projects can be accomplished with a basic collection of hand tools, solvents, strippers, and finishes. Basic hand tools that you probably already own will help you make most of the necessary structural repairs before refinishing. You'll also need some glue, clamps, and readily available solvents for cleaning and surface preparation.

Of course, if you have woodworking equipment and the skills to build new parts, you'll be able to tackle a broader range of projects. But in this book, I focus on using basic tools and supplies to do the kind of projects you'll most often encounter.

In this chapter, I discuss the proper personal safety equipment and the best place to work. Materials related to specific tasks, such as stains, sandpaper, and finishes are discussed in later chapters.

Hand tools

You may already have most of the hand tools you need, or you can buy them at a hardware store or home center. You may need some specialized tools for specific tasks.

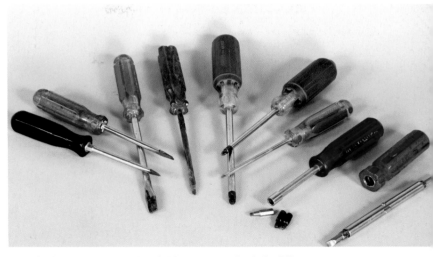

Flat-, Phillips-, and square-head drivers are available in different sizes. The compact multitip driver at the right has two sizes of Phillips- and flat-head tips.

Screwdrivers

You'll need an assortment of flat-, square-, and Phillips®-head screwdrivers. Older furniture usually has screws that require a flat-head driver. It's best to have a range of screwdriver sizes from a small (³/₃₂ in.) up to a ³/₈ in. If you try to remove a tight flat-head screw with a screwdriver blade that's too loose, you'll damage the slot making the screw impossible to remove. Just in case, I always keep a couple of old screwdrivers that can be custom-ground on a bench grinder for a snug fit in the screw head.

For newer furniture, you'll need at least two different size Phillips-head drivers. Phillips-head drivers are numbered #0 through #5 (small to large). I recommend #1 and #3. You may also run into square-drive screws, which are often used on foreign-made furniture. You can use a power drill, if you wish, but for brass screws on hinges and other hardware, using a hand driver is less likely to damage the soft brass.

workSmart

To make sure you're prepared for most situations where you'll need a screwdriver, buy a kit with a drive handle and assorted blade types and sizes.

The kit on the left has just about every size screwdriver tip. The tool on the right comes with several sizes of Phillips-, flat-, and square-heads.

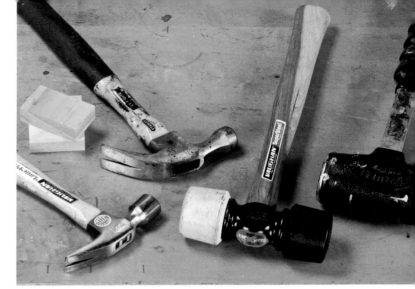

A standard claw hammer (left) should be used with soft wood blocks to protect the wood from damage. The rubber-faced ones can be used without a block.

A painter's multiscraper (top, center) is my favorite tool. Putty knives and spatulas in various sizes, a standard pocket knife, and a mat knife are also useful.

Remove the sharp edges of a new putty knife before using it with stripper.

Hammers

Claw hammers can drive and sometimes remove nails and are available in different weights. Buy one that feels comfortable in your hand. I prefer smaller hammers as I find they have better control. A rubber-faced mallet is good for knocking apart furniture joints. Try to get a deadblow mallet weighted with metal shot to avoid marring surfaces.

Scrapers and putty knives

A painter's scraper (see middle photo at left) is one of my most often used multipurpose tools. Its hefty blade can be used for both scraping and prying. The blade offers several edges to suit different shapes—half-round, angled, and straight—so you can scrape paint or glue off of just about anything. It can be reground easily with a file or a bench grinder. Putty knives in different widths are very useful. I suggest a wide blade (3 in.) and a narrow blade (1 in.) Round off the edges of the putty knife's blade with sandpaper to avoid damaging your project.

Pliers

The three essential pliers are standard, side cutting, and needle nose. End nippers are handy for cutting small nails and brads to smaller sizes. If you can find an inexpensive pair of end nippers that you don't mind grinding, you can make a great pulling and prying tool for nails and other fasteners (see "A specialized nail puller" on the facing page).

A variety of pliers is useful in refinishing work and furniture repair. Electrician's side cutters and end nippers (far right) aren't common household tools but are indispensable when dismantling furniture.

A specialized nail puller

You can modify end nippers to make an efficient tool for pulling nails. The curved face of this tool rarely leaves any marks on the wood or finish. Use a bench grinder to grind down the outside face of the tool. Grind the material away gradually to avoid overheating the metal. Follow the natural curve of the nippers. If there isn't a preground curve, add a slight curve as you grind. This curve will keep the tool from marring the wood. Grind until there's no outside bevel left and the two arms of the nipper are flush, as shown.

Use the tool to pull out nails or staples that are flush or slightly above the surface. Grasp the fastener and gently rock the tool handle downward to pull the nail or staple up a bit. Then grab the fastener closer to the surface of the wood and rock the handle down until the fastener comes out.

The end nippers on the right have been reground on a bench grinder until there's no bevel visible.

To use the modified end nippers, grab the nail and pull it up by rocking the tool down.

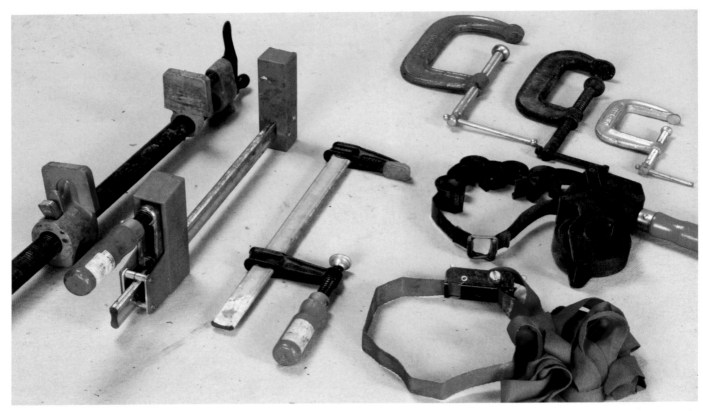

Some of the most common clamps you'll need for doing structural repairs: pipe and bar clamps (left), C-clamps (upper right), and band clamps (lower right), which are typically used to clamp frames and round or irregular-shaped items.

workSmart

Temporarily glue small pieces of wood to your C-clamps; otherwise you'll fumble with the clamp and the protectors when using glue that sets quickly. For pipe clamps, purchase the rubber protectors that slip over the jaws or make wooden ones as shown.

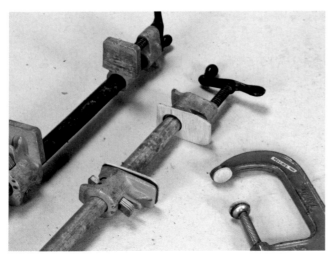

Clamps

If you do any woodworking, you probably have quite a few clamps. If you don't, you may need to purchase clamps for holding parts together during repair. Woodworkers have a saying, "You can never have enough clamps," but for general repairs, it's better to have the right clamp to do the job at hand.

C-clamps

A traditional clamp that you'll find in most hardware stores, the C-clamp is nothing more than a cast-metal body in the shape of a large C. The top of the C is shaped into a flat pad, while the other end has a threaded rod to which a sliding lever is attached. C-clamps are available in many sizes, from several inches to about a foot in length. A C-clamp longer than a foot is inefficient and unwieldy. For longer clamping spans, bar clamps are a better choice.

The metal pads on C-clamps will leave indentations on wood, so use them with wooden or plastic protectors to prevent marks. While useful to clamp small parts, C-clamps always need to be used with cauls to distribute clamping pressure, and they have a limited reach.

Bar and pipe clamps

Bar and pipe made up of clamps are available in many different lengths and jaw capacities. They are three parts: a stationary jaw with a crank or handle, a rigid bar or pipe, and a moveable jaw that rides on the bar or pipe. To use this type of clamp, unscrew (or uncrank) the handle all the way and place the bar (or pipe) across the width of the piece to be clamped. Then move up the sliding jaw to snug the clamp and tighten the screw at the other end to apply the clamping pressure.

Bar clamps are usually sold as a complete unit. The length is determined by the manufacturer. Pipe clamps are usually sold as two jaws that attach to iron plumbing pipe available at home centers and most hardware stores. The advantage of pipe clamps is that you can make clamps any length you wish. The pipe is very rigid and strong, which is why pipe clamps are so often used for regluing in furniture repair.

Band and strap clamps

A band clamp is nothing more than a fabric belt that wraps around the object you want to clamp, whether it is round, square, or irregular in shape. One end has a ratcheting mechanism and a loop that you pass the other end through, much like you would put a belt on around your waist. The ratchet end is then tightened so that pressure is distributed equally across the entire distance. This is a very effective way to clamp items like chairs and picture frames, because equal pressure is applied to all the joints simultaneously. Although you won't need them for every project, band clamps are inexpensive and worth having on hand.

Improvising a clamp

There are many clamping situations where you'll have to improvise. With bar clamps, you can create longer clamps (to clamp a sofa frame, for example) by hooking

To extend the reach of a bar clamp, use a coupler to connect the two ends.

The little piece of wood that split off the foot of this cabinet was too small and awkward to clamp. Masking tape worked perfectly.

the sliding jaws together. You could also convert two pipe clamps into a longer clamp by installing a pipe coupler between the two threaded ends.

Other items useful as clamps for complicated profiles and shapes can be found around the house. I've used masking tape, electrical tape, large rubber bands, shrink wrap, and even old inner tubes. Just about anything that's elastic will work.

You can get the inexpensive, disposable brushes (right) in bulk packs for discounted pricing. The better-quality brushes on the left are for applying finishes.

These are the most common types of rags used for refinishing. The textured, terry-cloth type (in the foreground) is better for stripping and cleaning, whereas the smoother textured microfiber and T-shirt materials are better for staining and finishing. When finishing, avoid rags that release lint.

Rags and brushes

Clean, absorbent cotton rags are a good choice for almost all refinishing tasks from cleaning to applying finishes. Generally I like textured terry cloth for cleaning finishes and using with strippers because the texture of the rag aids in cleaning. For applying stains and finishes, a smooth texture T-shirt fabric is preferred. If you like paper towels, they can be substituted for light cleaning and application of some finishes, but they break down and shred if you use them for heavy-duty tasks like stripping.

Have a selection of brushes on hand. Cheap 1-in. to 3-in. throw-away chip brushes are good for applying stripper and stain. You'll need a selection of quality finishing brushes (1 in. to 3 in. in width) for applying finishes. Use natural-bristle brushes for applying solvent-based products like oil stains and varnishes. Synthetic-bristle brushes are better suited for water-based products.

Safety equipment

Solvents and strippers strong enough to remove a finish can do serious harm to your skin, eyes, and lungs. When using any stripper, particularly those containing methylene chloride, work outside whenever possible. If you must work indoors, use a nonflammable stripper. Citrus-

Chemical-resistant gloves are almost always made from rubber or nitrile. Never use disposable gloves when working with stripper.

Always use thick, chemical-resistant gloves that cover your wrists and forearms when working with strippers and strong solvents.

or soy-based products are good for this purpose. Make sure to work in a large area with plenty of ventilation, such as a garage with the door open.

There are several types of particulate and vapor masks available to protect your lungs. For sanding wood, a well-fitting dust mask is adequate. But you'll need more to protect your lungs from harmful vapors. A good all-around mask is an organic vapor cartridge-style respirator with paper prefilters. This mask will protect you from particulate sanding dust as well as from vapors from solvents and most strippers and finishing products.

Protect your skin with solvent-resistant gloves when working with solvents, some glues and stains, and finishes. When working with strippers, wear gloves that cover your wrists and forearms. Wear safety goggles that seal tightly to your skin to protect your eyes from stripper and solvent splashes.

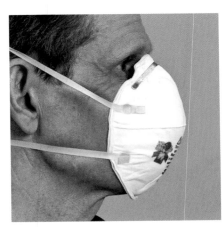

A dust mask will protect you from only sanding dust and other particulates.

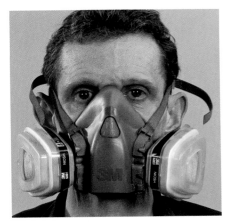

A paint and pesticide (organic vapor cartridge) mask will protect you from harmful vapors as well as dust.

These safety glasses wrap around your face and seal tightly to keep harmful liquids out of your eyes.

Glues

For the kind of structural repair work detailed in the next chapter, there are only three glues you'll need: premixed animal hide glue (we'll refer to it as hide glue), yellow carpenter's glue, and in some situations epoxy. Animal hide glue is a good choice for furniture made before 1940, but yellow carpenter's glue can be used for any repair as long as the joint is clean and the wood will accept glue. Epoxy is used when the wood parts don't fit back together well, or when the parts have been reglued poorly from a prior repair attempt.

Solvents

Solvents are used in refinishing for cleaning and reviving finishes, rinsing the residue from stripped furniture, and when thinning finishing materials and cleaning up. All the solvents I use can be purchased locally from paint and hardware stores and home centers. Strippers are discussed in detail in Chapter 5.

The most common glues for furniture repair are hide glue, yellow glue, and epoxy. They can be purchased at any hardware store or home center.

The wood on this leg had split where the apron bolt attaches. A poor regluing attempt means the joints will fit poorly and standard glues won't adhere properly, so I used two-part epoxy to make the repair.

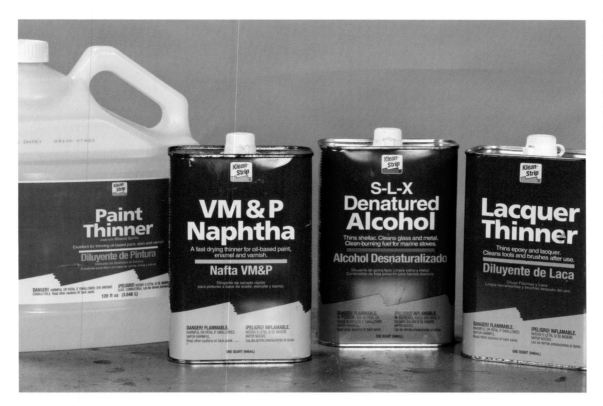

Mineral spirits, paint thinner, and naphtha

The three most common solvents have different names but they perform in similar ways. They're used for cleaning old finishes because they will remove oil-based dirt and grime as well as old polishes and waxes without damaging the finish. Paint thinner is almost identical to mineral spirits except for the cost, so they are interchangeable. Naphtha is sold as VM&P naphtha (varnish makers and paint naphtha) and works like the other solvents but dries much faster. I typically like paint thinner or mineral spirits for cleaning finishes because it doesn't evaporate so fast. Naphtha is useful for removing old tape and felt-tip pen marks.

Denatured alcohol

Denatured alcohol is used to thin shellac, clean bare wood, and serve as a rinse for stripper residue. It evaporates very quickly and does not have an objectionable odor. It's also used in reviving old shellac finishes. Because it is a solvent for shellac, denatured alcohol should never be used to clean an existing finish because it may damage it.

Lacquer thinner

Lacquer thinner is the best product for rinsing stripper residue and is also used in reviving old lacquer finishes. It should never be applied to an existing finish because it will remove most clear finishes and paint.

Structural repairs

efore refinishing or reviving a finish, you need to make your furniture structurally sound. Some professionals recommend making repairs after stripping due to the possibility that the stripper might deactivate the glues used in repairs. In my own work, I prefer to do repairs first, and I recommend that you do the same. It's much easier to wipe glue off of finished or even partially finished surfaces. Plus it's easier to mark and keep track of various parts. As long as you have good wood-to-wood contact when you reglue, the joint won't loosen during stripping. Further, the chances of stripper getting into poorly glued joints is really a big issue only in the pro shops, where they submerge furniture in stripper chemicals to remove the finish.

Diagnostics

To properly repair a furniture joint that's loose, you'll need to diagnose the extent of the problem. The easiest way to do this is to rack or twist the piece and see where the joinery is loose (see Chapter 1). Then examine the wood around the joint to see if there are hidden nails, screws, or other fasteners such as angle braces installed in a prior repair attempt. Screws will sometimes be hidden by screw-hole covers, which can be pried off. Put the

One of the most common problems in older solid wood furniture is a split that's the result of expansion and contraction over the years. It's an easy fix but requires taking the top off.

screws or other fasteners you'll need to reassemble the piece together in a safe place. For nails that are deeply embedded, you may need to remove some of the wood around them to pry them out. Putty can fill in for any missing wood later.

As you dismantle something, keep all the screws and other fasteners in one place so you can reuse them.

You might create a very complicated puzzle for yourself unless you mark the individual parts.

This joint wasn't going to come apart until the embedded nail was removed. Use a knife or small chisel to remove wood until you can grab the nail with pliers.

workSmart

Once all the pieces are apart, scrape off the large hunks of dried glue and use clean water to wash off the surfaces to be reglued. The parts should fit under moderate hand pressure. If you can wiggle them more than a couple of inches in either direction, you'll need to rebuild them with new wood and refit.

Dismantling

Though it may seem easy to remember how the piece goes back together, mark all the parts to indicate their position before dismantling. You can use a numbering sequence that's keyed to a diagram, but my favorite method is to write the name of the part and its position on masking tape. Be as specific as the complexity of the piece requires. For example: "top stretcher, right." Also, indicate orientation (like "up," "back").

If the joint was already loose and you've removed all fasteners, it should come apart easily. If not, a gentle whack with a rubber mallet will get it apart. If any joint fails to come apart with these techniques, I'd suggest getting the other parts apart as much as possible and regluing the stubborn joints by working glue into the joint as best you can with a toothpick, small brush, or thin piece of wood.

Probably the first dismantling job you'll run into is a chair, and because it's a small, easy to manage item, we'll use one as an example at the end of this chapter (see "Dismantling a chair," on p. 32).

Assembly

Assemble the furniture in the reverse order that you disassembled it. Do this on a level surface (like a tablesaw or level workbench). Have some warm, clean water and rags handy. Go through a dry-clamping assembly before applying the glue to make sure all the parts fit back together correctly. I recommend that you use hide glue if you have a complex assembly because it has a long open time. Otherwise, yellow (carpenter's) glue will work fine. Using the appropriate glue, apply it to both parts of the joint and clamp in stages. For example, glue together and temporarily clamp the front and back leg sections as separate units, then glue the units together.

When everything is assembled, tighten all the clamps and make sure the item is on a level surface. Check for wobbling. If the piece wobbles, you can force it back into square by skewing the clamps and retightening them until the wobble is gone. You may have to play with several of the clamps before the piece is steady.

Always glue items on a level surface like the top of a workbench.
A tablesaw or a large flat piece of plywood will also work.

workSmart

If your furniture is clamped and sitting on a known level surface but still wobbles, try angling one of the clamps up or down about 5°. You'll see the wobble either get worse or stabilize, depending on which way you angle the clamp.

Principles of regluing

The majority of repairs to furniture involve regluing. Glued joints fail for a variety of reasons: the reaction of the wood to seasonal humidity changes, internal stress in the wood, ordinary wear and tear, an accident, or negligence.

The first repair you'll probably ever run into may be something as simple as a loose rung on a chair or as seemingly complex as a bookcase that's falling apart. Whatever the gluing operation may be, there are two basic requirements:

• Clean wood surfaces so the new glue can penetrate.

• Good wood-to-wood contact for the joint to last.

All successful gluing operations must meet these conditions or the joint will fail.

If you apply glue to a joint that has old glue, dirt, or polishes, it will never stick. Here, I'm wiping the gluing surfaces with distilled water after scraping and sanding the wood clean.

Before applying the glue, check the fit without glue to make sure it's snug and has good wood-to-wood contact.

Sometimes cracks won't open up enough to allow you to apply glue with a brush, so you must improvise. Here, I'm using an artist's palette knife to get the glue into the crack.

A prior attempt to make a repair with a finish nail won't allow this break to close for proper gluing. Before attempting to reglue, I must remove the nail.

Breaks, cracks, and splits

Cracks and splits are handled differently, depending on whether the crack will close under nominal pressure. If it's a recent split or crack due to accidental stress or breakage, it should close easily with hand pressure or light clamping. In this case, the repair is a simple matter of introducing the correct glue and clamping. If the crack or split does not close easily, it may be caused by seasonal movement or internal drying that stressed the

wood. Or it might be an old break that wasn't repaired when it should have been. Sometimes the splinters from the break become rearranged in a way that prevents the crack from reclosing. Or there may be hidden hardware from a prior repair pinning the wood in position.

If the crack does not close, check first for splinters. Use a small knife to poke around. Try to pull out any splinters you find. Also look for any nails or screws from a prior repair attempt. Dry-assemble the joint (without

The two smaller clamps press the part flat, while the long bar clamp clamps the break together. This way the repair will be almost invisible.

The crack in this leg wouldn't close completely so I used epoxy, which will also stick to the old glue used in a prior gluing attempt. Note the clamps used on the sides to keep it aligned.

To clamp this bracket foot, I made a pine caul shaped to the foot so the clamps have a flat bearing surface on both ends.

Broken dowels can be easily replaced with new ones.

glue) and apply clamps until you're satisfied that the gap is completely closed. You may have to use several clamps, applying pressure in more than one direction, to get the opening completely closed. If the damaged section is irregularly shaped, you may need to make wood cauls shaped to the part.

Once you know you can close the gap, apply glue to the crack. Reclamp and wipe off the glue squeeze-out with a water-dampened cloth (hide or yellow glue) or denatured alcohol (epoxy). Set the piece aside to dry and periodically wipe away glue, as it will continue to seep out slightly until the glue cures. Remove the clamps after the recommended setting time for the glue.

When the crack won't close

If the split or crack won't close completely, get it to close as best you can and use epoxy to glue it. Epoxies are gap filling and will do a better job then yellow or hide glue. Clean off the excess epoxy with denatured alcohol. When you clamp, tighten the clamp just enough to get a little squeeze-out because epoxies require a somewhat thick glueline.

Dowels

Dowels are short pieces of round wood that are used to join wood parts together. Modern dowels are grooved and compressed, both to allow an escape for glue

squeeze-out and to let them swell a bit, forming a tight connection. If you have a broken or loose dowel you can usually remove it; you may have to drill it out. Then replace it with a new dowel. To do this correctly typically requires full or partial dismantling.

workSmart

Purchase ready-made dowels, which can be found in some hardware stores and home centers or online woodworking retailers. Dowel rods are my second choice because they're usually slightly undersize.

Regluing a top

This small table has a typical problem—the top has split along the old glue joint.

1. **Remove the top.** The screws that hold the top to the base will prevent the clamps from closing the open joint, so you'll need to take the top off. Notice how the top comes off in two pieces.

2. **Scrape off all the old glue.**

3. **Sand the joint** with 120-grit sandpaper using a long block of wood to help stabilize the sandpaper and to prevent deforming the edge. Clean off the debris with clean water. Do a quick test-clamp (without glue) to check that the fit is snug.

4. **Apply a thin bead of glue** using your finger to spread it.

5. **Clamp the top together** using pipe or strong bar clamps. The glue sometimes makes the two parts slip out of position, so use two clamps on either end to get the top perfectly flat.

Repairing broken wood

When I tried to take apart this joint, I damaged it, thanks to a hidden nail.

1. **Pull the break apart** and check for any nails or splinters and remove them.

2. **Dry-clamp** the pieces (without glue) to make sure they will fit tightly.

3. **Apply glue** to the fresh wood that's been exposed. Keep the glue off any surfaces that will be glued later.

4. **Use two pieces of wood as cauls** to distribute the clamping pressure and use wax paper under the cauls so they don't get glued to the wood. Wipe away the squeeze-out with a damp rag.

5. **Check frequently** (about every 5 minutes) and wipe away any additional glue seepage.

Repairing a split or crack

If the wood hasn't broken apart enough to expose a fresh gluing surface, you'll need a slightly different approach.

1. **Open the crack** as wide as you can and use a thin piece of wood or metal or an artist's palette knife to work some glue into the crack.

2. **Use a clamp, if you can.** Many times cracks like these are hard to clamp because the surfaces are uneven. In this case, I used electrical tape, and wrapped it around several times, pulling tight with each overlap.

3. **Proceed with any other necessary repairs.** The advantage of the tape is that it allows you to continue working while the glue in the crack dries. Tape doesn't get in the way as a clamp would.

Replacing a glue block

Missing glue blocks are a common problem on pieces like cabinets. Glue blocks provide strength and support to parts vulnerable to stress such as the bases of chests.

1. **Repair any broken parts.** If you see any broken feet on a piece like this nightstand, you can bet that the break was caused by a missing glue block. In this case, someone simply tried to nail on the broken part.

2. **Use the glue outline** from the original block to size the new block. For this block, I used a scrap of pine 2×4.

3. **Scrape off the old glue** from the area where you'll glue the new block and apply glue.

4. **Glue on the new block.** You'll need two clamps. Make sure you use clamps with protective pads so you don't damage the finish on the exterior.

Dismantling a chair

This wobbly, old chair was made using mortise-and-tenon construction. There were nails in almost every joint. Always look for hidden nails if a joint doesn't come apart easily, otherwise you'll damage the piece even further.

1. **Mark all the parts** using masking tape. Make sure you use "left," "right," "top," etc.

2. **Remove all visible fasteners** such as screws from the glue blocks. If you see a screw-hole cover like the one here, pry it off to expose the screw.

3. **Gently tap stubborn parts** with a rubber-faced mallet. Glue blocks may need a gentle whack with a hammer to break the glue joint.

4. **Try to take the joints apart** by hand, wiggling a little. If necessary, use a rubber hammer.

5. **Check for hidden fasteners** if the joints don't release, especially hidden nails. You may have to remove some wood around the nail to pry it out.

6. **Take the chair apart in stages;** for example, take the front legs and stretchers off first, then the side rails. After that, you can take apart the back legs, seat rail, the crest, the splat, and so on.

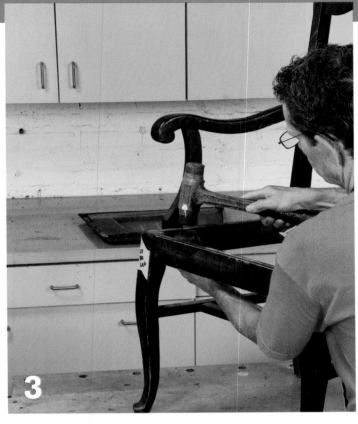

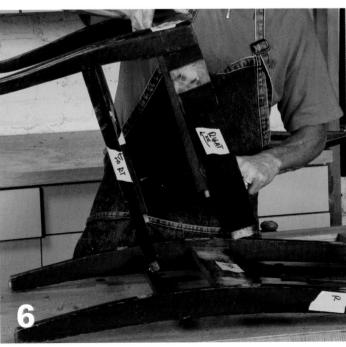

Assembling a chair

eassemble the chair in the reverse order in which you took it apart, creating subassemblies. Get your clamps, glue, and other materials ready in advance so you don't have to look for them after the glue is spread.

1. **Repair any cracks or splits,** whether the result of hard use or from the dismantling process.

2. **Clean off the glue** you can see on the wood surfaces and then wipe well around the joints using a rag and water.

3. **Put the piece back together using logical** subassemblies. In this case, I reassembled the back legs, seat rail, crest, and back splat first. Then I reassembled the front legs and stretcher.

4. **Allow the glue in the subassemblies to set** for an hour or longer. Then remove the clamps and assemble the chair. Attach the front to the back using the side rails. Make sure you do this on a level surface and check that the chair doesn't wobble. If it does, you can correct the wobble by angling the clamps to compensate.

5. **Install the glue blocks last,** using glue and the original screws.

Cleaning and reviving

Some antiques experts say that old furniture should never be stripped of the original finish because it diminishes the value. They argue that preserving a part of history allows analysis of old finishes and the methods for applying them. And stripping robs old furniture of the patina, or old look, that most people find attractive. If you have a truly valuable antique, you may want to consult an expert, but if the existing finish is in good shape, you could clean and revive the finish, which usually doesn't affect its worth. These techniques are used extensively in the antiques and museum trades. Because you're not removing the existing finish, you're not exposed to the harsher chemicals used in stripping.

In this chapter, I explain which finishes respond well to cleaning and reviving techniques and which don't. I also show you several no-strip methods. You can try them on any furniture (even new pieces) to see how they work. If you don't like the result, you can always strip the piece later without having invested a lot of time.

This drop-front desk is in good shape except for the finish, which looks a little dull. There are also some minor scratches and dirt around the drawer. This is an excellent candidate for two-step cleaning followed by waxing.

Finishes that can be cleaned and revived

The best finishes to clean and revive are old shellac and lacquer finishes. Modern finishes like polyurethanes and waterborne finishes can be cleaned, but they don't respond well to waxing or reviving with solvents or finishes. Painted finishes also aren't good candidates, but sometimes just using the cleaning technique discussed next can improve the look of an old painted finish as well as newer waterborne finishes and polyurethanes.

Ideally the finish should be in good shape, which you can usually tell just by looking at it. If you can see distinct wood grain or figure and there's some luster to the finish, it's probably in good enough shape to try cleaning or reviving. You can run a simple series of elimination tests with solvents to determine if the finish is shellac, lacquer, or something else. This will save you a bit of frustration and also helps in determining the right stripper if you decide to go that way (see "Testing a finish with solvents" on p. 44).

Finish problems that require stripping

If your furniture has any of the following problems, you should consider going straight to stripping, unless you're sure the piece is valuable or you may want to sell it in the future.

A. **Missing finish.** Missing finish is usually obvious, but sometimes it's hard to spot, particularly if the original finish is very thin. Wiping the finish with mineral spirits is helpful if you're not sure. The missing area will darken while the finish remaining on the surface will appear lighter.

B. **Black or gray areas.** Cleaning and reviving will not remove black or gray areas. These problems indicate damage to the wood underneath and not the finish. An exception is small areas around metal fasteners or hardware, which may add some character if you leave them alone.

C. **Large scratches and gouges.** Long, deep scratches and gouges may be through the finish and penetrate to soft wood below. Cleaning and reviving may actually accentuate these and make them look worse.

D. **Sticky finishes.** Finishes that are routinely handled or in contact with skin will become sticky over time. You'll see this around pulls and knobs on drawers and cabinet doors as well as on the arms of chairs. Sticky finishes have become chemically altered and they remain soft and tacky. If you press a Q-tips® or piece of tissue on the finish and parts of the Q-tips or tissue remain, go right to stripping because even after cleaning, the finish will remain tacky. If you apply a new finish over it, it won't harden.

E. **Alligatored finishes.** Some finishes that have been applied thickly will become brittle and crack as they get older and show lighter areas underneath, almost like little islands. Pros call this *alligatored* because the resulting finish is rough and resembles bumpy alligator skin. Pass on trying to clean or revive these finishes.

F. **Brittle, peeling, or cloudy finish.** Old finishes that can be easily chipped or flaked off with a fingernail should be stripped. Pieces exposed to moisture or water for extended periods of time will have white cloudy areas and should also be stripped.

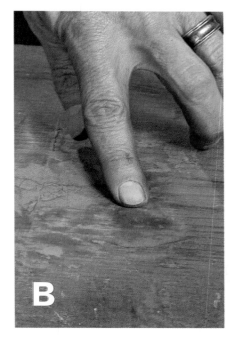

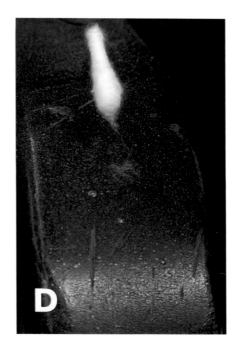

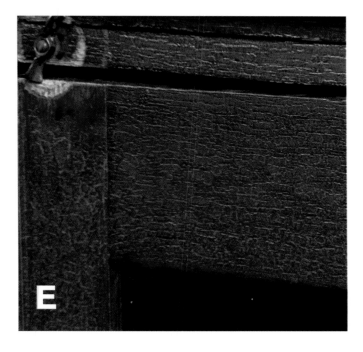

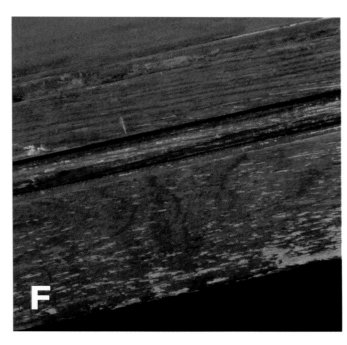

Begin the cleaning process with paint thinner, mineral spirits, or naphtha.

Clean first, then decide

There are several techniques to reviving a finish. But they all start with a thorough cleaning. Cleaning techniques do not remove finish or involve the use of strippers. Before using reviving techniques that involve applying solvents or finish over the old finish, start with a good cleaning and waxing. See how you like the result. If cleaning doesn't achieve the look you want, you can try one of the reviving methods using solvents or finish.

Materials for cleaning

Cleaning is a two-step process that removes both water- and oil-soluble dirt and grime. For the first step, you'll need some basic materials. Mineral spirits and paint thinner remove oily dirt, old wax, and polish. VM&P naphtha is a faster-evaporating form of mineral spirits.

warning

Protect your lungs by wearing a solvent-rated respirator when using paint thinner or mineral spirits.

You can work faster because you don't need to wait as long for it to dry. I prefer to use paint thinner or mineral spirits because they stay wet longer.

You'll also need some warm water and Dawn® detergent (the blue-colored original is best) for the second step. You'll also need some absorbent rags, ideally with a little texture (like a terry-cloth towel) to help pull grime off. If the grime doesn't come off with the cloth, you can use 0000 steel wool, but go very lightly and don't overwork it or you'll go through the finish.

Two-step cleaning

The first step removes old waxes and oil-based grime such as grease. Always wear a respirator when using petroleum-based solvents.

Don't be surprised if you don't see a lot of grime on your rag. That means the finish probably wasn't waxed often or was exposed to oil-based products. Most of the grime and dirt will be removed in the second step because of the degreasing action of the detergent in the water. This helps pull off the oily film and residue from the first step. The water also removes water-soluble grime (like sugary food spills). Lightly wiping afterward with distilled water removes any soap residue. When it's dry, you can decide if you want to proceed to the next step—waxing.

Wax is the final step

A coat or two of paste wax really makes a difference after cleaning. Not only does it add a bit of luster but it gives old pieces that silky feel well-cared-for old furniture acquires over time.

Furniture paste wax comes in clear and tinted versions, for use on darker woods. If you deliberately leave a little dark wax in corners and crevices, it imparts an antiqued look.

Reviving a finish

A finish that looks dull or frosty is probably *crazed*. Crazing is fine cracks in the finish that are the result of the finish aging and becoming brittle. The cracks develop when the wood expands and contracts due to seasonal fluctuations in humidity. Cleaning and waxing won't help this type of problem, but you can try reviving the finish, which may diminish the crazing effect and put more luster into the finish. If you think or know the piece is valuable, stick with the cleaning and waxing process described earlier. Use revivers on lacquer and shellac finishes only. Test an inconspicuous area (see "Testing a finish with solvents" on p. 44) before using a reviver.

Solvent-based revivers

Use solvent-based revivers when you have fine crazing, chips, or scratches. The added-color in these products hides some of the damage, while the strong solvents soften the finish slightly, which can remedy other problems like white marks from glasses. These products are especially good for legs and bases, where finishes get the most wear and tear.

Unfortunately, solvent revivers are a quick-fix solution, and the instant improved appearance doesn't last. The best use of these products is to color minor scratches and fix problems like white rings. If you want a long-term result and a better-looking surface, consider applying a finish reviver.

Tinted wax

Tinted wax is available from finishing and woodworking suppliers. Always use tinted paste waxes on dark wood or dark-stained finishes. If you use the untinted wax (sold as natural or clear), it sometimes dries leaving a whitish residue, which looks particularly bad on open-grained woods like oak.

This old mirror has a dull, lifeless finish but it's doesn't feel rough and there's some nice oak grain poking through. This is a great candidate for reviving with finish.

A solvent-based reviver with a dark color is a great quick fix for the wear and tear on this table leg.

Using solvent revivers

Clean the piece with the two-step cleaning method as described previously. Lightly sand the old finish with 400-grit sandpaper and remove the dust. Then apply the reviver. After about an hour, you should see an improved surface. You can apply a second coat if you wish. If you want a little more depth and luster, you can apply several coats of wax.

It's not a good idea to put a clear finish over these products because the finish may not adhere properly. If you don't like the effect of the reviver, let it dry for several days. Then clean the piece with the two-step process. After it's dry, try reviving using a finish.

Reviving using finish

If testing indicates the finish is shellac or lacquer, you can apply highly thinned finish to "reflow" it. This will disguise the crazing and improve luster. If the finish is varnish, you'll need to use a slightly different technique.

Clean the finish with the two-step process described earlier, except on a known lacquer finish substitute TSP (or TSP substitute) cleaner for the Dawn detergent to remove silicone from the surface, which could cause fisheye (see "Removing fisheye" on p. 104). After drying, sand as much of the crazing away with 400-grit nonclogging sandpaper as possible without cutting through the finish. Nonclogging sandpaper is generically called *stearated* sandpaper (two trade names are Norton 3X and 3M™ Fre-Cut™). The sandpaper will eventually load up with hard "corns," so check it frequently and switch to a fresh piece when you see buildup. Remove the dust. Use the correct method for the specific existing finish, as follows.

Shellac Thin 1 part shellac with 3 parts denatured alcohol. Using a bristle brush, flow this mixture onto the surface trying to use long strokes, not a quick back-and-forth method. Let the mix dry 1 hour. Sand lightly with 400-grit sandpaper. Then apply the shellac at normal strength, typically a 2-lb. cut. Three coats are usually sufficient for a good appearance.

Lacquer Thin 1 part brushing lacquer with 3 parts lacquer thinner. Test this in an inconspicuous spot by brushing a small area. If you see a fisheye appearance,

Crazing vs. alligatoring

Don't confuse crazing with an alligatored finish (see p. 38). If you look closely at the finish with lighting behind, you can see the cracks just on the surface. The crazing should not go all the way through the finish or appear darker or lighter than the overall color.

The old shellac finish on this mirror can be revived by sanding, applying thinned shellac, and then waxing.

As you sand old finish, look at the sandpaper frequently for hard "corns." These will cause more damage by gouging the finish.

stop and add some fisheye eliminator to the thinned lacquer in the recommended amount. Fisheye eliminator is available from finishing supply retailers or from automotive refinishing stores. Apply the thinned lacquer to the crazed area. If possible, keep the surface horizontal, so the lacquer doesn't run or drip. Let it dry for 4 hours to 6 hours. Sand with 400-grit sandpaper and then apply another coat, if necessary. After drying and sanding, apply two more coats of lacquer at full strength.

Varnish Sand as much of the crazing off as you can without sanding through to bare wood or the stain, remove the dust, and then apply several coats of oil-based wiping varnish. Don't use the thinned varnish because varnish won't soften with any type of solvent added.

When reflowing crazed lacquer finishes, the thinned lacquer is applied as heavily as you can, so keep the working surface horizontal, if possible.

Testing a finish with solvents

Before cleaning or reviving a finish, use a simple test to identify the finish. Always test in an area that won't be noticeable because some solvents will soften the finish.

1. **Find an inconspicuous area to test.** Good spots are behind hardware, the undersides of a table, and the bottom in an unseen area. Pick an area that seems to have a good build of finish on it.

2. **Put a small puddle of denatured alcohol** on a horizontal surface and wait a couple of minutes.

3. **Tap your finger** where you applied the alcohol to see if the finish has turned sticky. This drawer front became very sticky, so the finish is shellac.

4. **If the finish doesn't get sticky,** repeat the test using lacquer thinner. If you want more control in the application, transfer the lacquer thinner to a small squeeze bottle or eyedropper bottle. If lacquer thinner makes the finish sticky, the finish is lacquer. If neither have any effect, the finish is varnish, polyurethane, or another type of modern finish.

Two-step cleaning

A thorough cleaning may be all that an old piece of furniture needs to look acceptable. Before reviving or stripping a finish, try cleaning.

1. **Dampen a clean cloth** with paint thinner or mineral spirits. Rub a small area in circles. Don't saturate the finish. Switch to a clean part of the cloth frequently. Go over the whole piece and let it dry.

2. **Put one capful of Dawn dishwashing detergent** in a pint of lukewarm water. Apply the solution with a dampened (not dripping wet) clean cloth, and rub a small area at a time. Turn the rag to a clean surface frequently as it loads up with grime.

3. **Wipe off all the excess fluid** with a rag dampened slightly with clean water. You should see a much improved surface, as shown on the desk front here. (The right side hasn't been cleaned yet.)

4. **Revisit any stubborn areas of grime** that the first or second steps haven't removed. You can rework that area as much as needed. The area around the drawer knob was very dirty, so I cleaned it again with detergent and water.

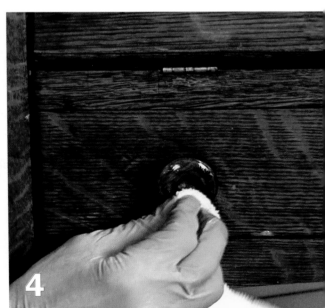

Waxing

Waxing, the last step in cleaning, gives furniture extra protection and imparts a silky feel to the touch.

1. **Put a scoop of wax inside a clean cloth.** Wrap the rag so you form a ball with wax inside.

2. **Apply the wax in a circular motion.** A dark wax, like I'm using here, also helps hide minor scratches and scrapes.

3. **Work the wax** into turned areas, carvings, and other irregular areas with a bristle brush (a shoe-shine brush works well).

4. **Wait for the wax to haze** (seen on the left half of the desk front). Drying to a haze typically takes anywhere from 5 minutes to 15 minutes.

5. **Use a clean cloth to buff the wax** to the shine you like. Because wax can dry quickly always work on a section you can manage. If the wax is hard to buff, sprinkle a small amount of mineral spirits on a rag and rework the wax.

Reviving
with solvent

This walnut table is a good candidate to revive with a colored solvent reviver. The finish is in relatively good shape, but there were a lot of light scrapes and chips. The color will hide the majority of surface imperfections.

1. **Saturate a cloth** with paint thinner or mineral spirits and clean the whole piece. Let dry. Then clean with detergent, using 1 capful of Dawn in 1 pint of lukewarm water. Wipe dry with a clean cloth. Allow the surface to dry completely.

2. **Sand the finish lightly** using 400-grit sandpaper. Remove the dust.

3. **Pour the solvent reviver on a clean rag** and apply it liberally to the surface. Wipe the excess off, taking care not to let the reviver sit or puddle.

4. **Check to see** if the improved surface, which should be immediately evident, is the look you want. If not, you can repeat the previous step or apply tinted wax to deepen the color.

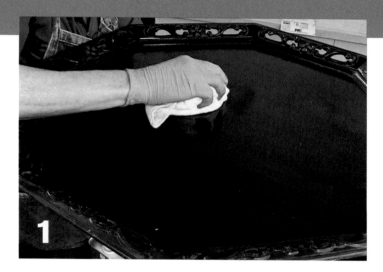

Reviving a crazed finish

Test the finish to make sure you're using the right product. Done correctly, this method leaves you with a finish that still looks old but has luster and shows the wood's figure.

1. **Clean using the two-step process.** Then sand flat areas with 400-grit sandpaper. Wipe away the dust periodically to check your progress.

2. **Go over the sanded areas with 0000 steel wool** as well as the areas you can't sand with sheet sandpaper. Remove the dust with a clean cloth.

3. **Dilute 1 part orange shellac** (a 3-lb. cut) with 3 parts denatured alcohol. Using a bristle brush, apply the mix as wet as you can without drips or runs. For a lacquer finish, use a mix of 1 part brushing lacquer to 3 parts lacquer thinner.

4. **After overnight drying, you should see a much improved surface and clarity to the grain.** You can stop here if you want a minimum build finish and simply rub it with some 0000 steel wool and paste wax.

5. **If you want a higher-build finish,** again sand it with 400-grit sandpaper and 0000 steel wool as in Steps 1 and 2, and repeat the shellac application using a mix of 1 part shellac to 1 part denatured alcohol. For lacquer, use 1 part brushing lacquer to 1 part lacquer thinner. Apply one to three more coats.

6. **Touch up any scrapes** by applying some dry furniture powder pigment mixed with the shellac or use a touch-up marker.

7. **The final result** is an attractive, smoother finish.

Removing
the finish

Many people jump right into stripping a finish only to find it's more work than they've bargained for. So the project gets put off or thrown out. I'm not going to tell you that stripping is fun, but it can be bearable and efficient if you understand the materials and especially which strippers work best for the finish you're trying to remove. Certain strippers work better on some finishes than on others, so you'll want to review the testing methods in the previous chapter.

Types of strippers

Strippers fall into three categories based on the chemicals they contain. Manufacturers must list chemical components that are hazardous. Unfortunately, the more efficient the stripper (which means it will remove the finish more quickly), the greater the level of hazard.

Methylene chloride

Methylene chloride has been the main ingredient in strippers for decades. It is the fastest and most efficient chemical for removing all types of finishes. Methylene chloride has two other advantages. It's nonflammable, and it works from the bottom up, meaning that it penetrates and swells the finish until it breaks free of the wood surface and can be removed cleanly and easily (see the photo on the facing page).

A typical methylene chloride–based stripper contains about 75% methylene chloride. The solution also contains methyl alcohol to help the methylene chloride penetrate faster, detergents to wet the surface of the finish,

There are basically three types of strippers available to consumers: traditional methylene chloride–based strippers (left), NMP-based "safe" strippers (foreground, right) and liquid refinishers composed of several solvents (background, right).

Methylene chloride–based stripper is my choice. It works the fastest and is usually the least expensive.

heat exposure may cause temperature of conditions, this may cause product to expand, c

If spilled, contain material and remove with absorbent, container and unused contents i regulations.

DISPOSAL: Clean up rags, papers and waste evaporate, then dispose of in metal container regulations.

CONTAINS: Methylene Chloride (CAS# 75-0 Spirits (CAS# 8052-41-3). Less than 200 gra non-photochemically reactive.

Liability is limited to refund of purchase price or

Formulated in USA since 1949. Packaged in C

For problems or

Look on the list of ingredients to see if methylene chloride is listed first. That means it's the main ingredient.

warning

Methylene chloride is a suspected carcinogen, and it evaporates very quickly, causing a rapid buildup of the vapors. Those fumes can rob anyone nearby of an adequate supply of oxygen. For that reason, people with heart problems are especially sensitive to such exposures and should not use methylene chloride strippers.

activators like alkalis (ammonia or lye), and paraffin wax dissolved in toluene to prevent the other solvents from evaporating too quickly.

Other than masks that supply air from an outside source, no standard respirators are rated to handle methylene chloride fumes. So the best place to use it is outdoors or in a well-ventilated area.

Liquid refinishers

Strippers sold as refinishers are effective only on lacquer and shellac finishes so you must know beforehand that you have one of those finishes (see "Testing a finish with solvents" on p. 44). They work from the top down by dissolving the finish layer-by-layer, and they work best when used with abrasive pads like steel wool.

They don't work very well on paint, and they have hardly any effect on varnishes. Because they evaporate quickly, you must keep the surface saturated, or the finish will reharden on the wood. Sometimes they contain a small amount of methylene chloride to give them some added kick.

Liquid refinishers are a blend of strong solvents like methyl alcohol, acetone, and toluene. They will dissolve shellac and lacquer finishes but have no affect on varnishes.

Nonflammable alternatives to methylene chloride and liquid refinishers are usually called "safe" strippers. They are usually based on the chemical *N*-methyl-pyrrolidone (NMP).

The downside with these strippers is that they are extremely flammable, so you must use them in a well-ventilated area and take the appropriate precautions. A cartridge-style respirator will properly filter the vapors, except for any methylene chloride that's added.

Safe strippers

The main active chemical in almost all safe formulations is the chemical *N*-methyl-pyrrolidone (NMP). Often sold as citrus-based strippers (they have a strong citrus scent from another chemical additive), these products provide an alternative to methylene chloride–based strippers. Some of these products are soy based. Products in this class work on all finishes.

NMP is still hazardous, but the vapors don't build up as much because the solution evaporates more slowly. This makes the stripper safer to use and keeps the surface wet and active for a longer time. Some versions come with a paper to lay over the stripper after application, which helps keep the stripper wet and active longer.

I use NMP-based strippers only when I must strip indoors. They cost significantly more than comparative methylene chloride strippers, and they take much longer to work.

Working with strippers

If possible, work outside to prevent the buildup of harmful fumes. Temperature affects the speed at which strippers work, so your project and working area should be as close to room temperature as possible.

Prepare the work area and collect any items you'll need so they will be close at hand. Be sure to wear the appropriate safety gear, including eye protection and a respirator, if appropriate. Have lots of rags handy both to remove the stripper and finish and to keep the work area clean.

When working with methylene chloride and NMP strippers, apply the stripper and let it do the work. Don't constantly work the surface or you'll need to apply many unnecessary additional coats of stripper. When the stripper is ready, the finish can be removed smoothly and easily.

Be prepared with a container into which you can dump the finish as you remove it. A cardboard box works well. To dispose of the sludge or finish–stripper residue, it's perfectly safe to spread it out onto some newspapers layered up in a shallow box and place it outside.

Let the stripper do the work! Most people are too anxious and as a consequence have to apply several coats of stripper. When you are removing the finish completely, there's hardly any friction felt with the putty knife.

Push the finish off one edge with the putty knife and into a waiting rag or cardboard box.

Twine will remove finish and paint from turned recesses.

On open-grained woods like oak, paint will remain in the grain and you need some special techniques to remove it. Small brass-bristle brushes are stiffer than nylon brushes and get down into the grain to work the softened paint out.

The solvents will evaporate and eventually you'll end up with a dried, crusty residue. It's then safe to throw it out, but only if it's a clear finish. For paint that may contain lead, call your municipality to see if there are special regulations for disposal.

Furniture stripped with methylene chloride and liquid refinishers is ready to finish in a day or so. Furniture stripped with one of the safe strippers will take between 3 and 7 days to dry before you can apply finishing materials. Try to keep the furniture as warm as possible. The furniture is ready to finish when the wood feels dry to the touch and sands without the sandpaper clogging up.

Stripping problems

Paint will remain in the pores of large-pored woods like oak unless the paint was applied over an existing clear finish. To get the paint out, remove as much of it as you can from the surface, then apply a generous coat of stripper and lay wax paper over the top. Let it sit until you see the paint in the pores start to "puff" out. Then use a brass-bristle brush to scrub the paint out. Stubborn paint can be picked out with a dental pick.

Intricate surfaces like turnings and carvings can be cleaned of finish effectively by several means. One is to wrap a piece of twine around turnings and pull it back and forth shoe-shine style to gently abrade the finish off. Planer chips used with a nylon brush can clean up carved areas very effectively, and a dental pick or sharpened piece of wood (use a pencil sharpener to put a point on a small-diameter dowel) can be used to clean small crevices and detailed areas. If you don't have a planer, try asking a cabinet shop to part with some shavings.

Helpful stripping accessories

Some common household items and tools are helpful in removing finishes during stripping.

• Dental picks and sharpened sticks can remove paint from cervices.

• Brass brushes can remove paint lodged in large-pored woods like oak.

• Twine helps clean up the grooves in turned parts.

• If you have a planer, save the chips. They're great for removing stripper residue and can be worked with a bristle brush to remove stripping sludge from carvings and other intricate areas.

• Synthetic (nylon) brushes are used to scrub away residue.

• Putty knives in various widths can lift finish up off the wood once the stripper has softened it. Sand the corners lightly so they don't dig into the wood.

• Steel wool and synthetic steel wool (Scotch-Brite®) are handy to scrub away finish; and, finally, have plenty of rags on hand.

Helpful for getting into details and crevices: pointed sticks and picks, twine, and brass-bristle brushes.

Putty knives, nylon-bristle brushes, and planer chips help remove finishes from wood.

Have a good supply of rags and steel wool.

Preparing to strip

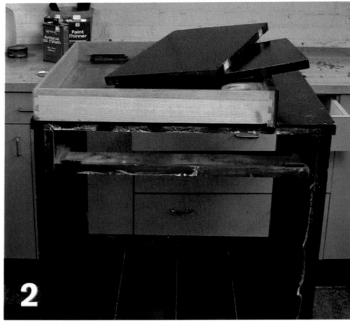

Stripping is a lot easier if you prepare beforehand. This checklist will get you started off in the right direction.

1. **Make any structural repairs** like this loose mortise and tenon joint first. Let the glue dry at least one day. As long as the repair has good wood-to-wood contact, the glue joint won't be affected by the stripper.

2. **Take the item apart as much as possible.** Start by removing all hardware, glass, and mirrors. Remove upholstery. Take tops (if they come off easily), backs, and legs off if you can.

3. **Wear appropriate clothing and safety equipment.** Use splash-proof eye protection and chemical-resistant gloves. Also wear long-sleeve shirts (thick flannel is best) and long pants. Don't leave any skin exposed. If possible, work outdoors.

4. **Place your project at a comfortable working height.** Sawhorses covered by a piece of plywood provide a good work surface. Although most strippers are a paste consistency, I like to orient the part I'm stripping so it's flat. Protect the area below with a tarp.

5. **Pour a generous amount of stripper** into a plastic painter's pail. Make a slit in the lid so you can leave the brush soaking in the stripper when you're not using it.

6. **Cover or put rags** where you don't want dripping stripper to cause a problem. One example is rags under holes for drawer hardware.

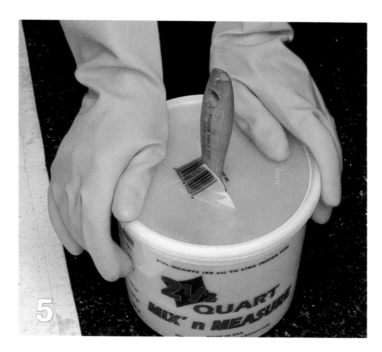

Using methylene chloride and NMP strippers

Methylene chloride and NMP strippers work in the same way, the difference being the time it takes for them to work. Methylene chloride strippers start to work almost immediately while NMP strippers may take several hours.

1. **Apply a generous amount of stripper** using a cheap brush. Don't brush back and forth; just try to apply it as thickly as you can without working it too much. Ideally, you want a thick, uniform coat of stripper.

2. **Depending on temperature,** wait about 10 minutes. Check to see if the finish is uniformly crinkled or bubbly. Try an area with a putty knife and see if the finish comes up. If it resists the putty knife, wait longer.

3. **Wait until the finish rolls off** without much resistance. But if you wait too long, the stripper and finish will dry, and you'll have to start all over again.

4. **Scrape the stripper–finish mix** off the putty knife into a cardboard box.

5. **Use steel wool to remove finish from recesses** like this groove.

6. **Clean off the residue with a rag** after the finish has been removed as much as possible. Textured rags like terry-cloth work the best. If you still see finish remaining, apply stripper again.

7. **Use a dowel** sharpened with a pencil sharpener to strip the hard-to-get-at places.

8. **Rinse the stripped wood** well with lacquer thinner.

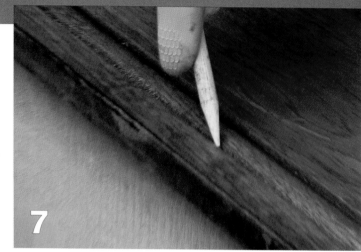

workSmart

You can speed up the dry time by repeated rinsing with lacquer thinner or denatured alcohol.

Using a liquid refinisher

Refinishers are a good choice if the item has an old lacquer or shellac finish, especially if you want to preserve the old color and character. You can use metal or synthetic steel wool but I prefer metal wool because it holds the liquid refinisher better.

1. **Pour refinisher** into a solvent-proof container.

2. **Dunk 00 steel wool into the refinisher** and apply it to the surface. Flood a workable area of the surface with refinisher.

3. **Let the refinisher work** for a minute or so. Then rub with the steel wool to remove the finish.

4. **Rinse the piece.** Although refinishers are a high-powered form of lacquer thinner, I always rinse anyway to find spots I may have missed.

workSmart

Rather than trying to strip the whole piece at once, work on one manageable part at a time, like a leg or a side, laying it flat, if possible.

Stripping paint

The best stripper to use for paint is heavy paste methylene chloride stripper, usually labeled "for paint and varnish."

1. **Select a manageable section** and lay the stripper on with a brush as thickly as you can.

2. **When the paint starts to blister,** test to see if it can be removed. Always try to wait as long as you can without the stripper drying out.

3. **Scrape the paint off** with a putty knife. You'll probably still see paint underneath so plan on applying a second or even third coat of stripper.

4. **Apply a final coat** after you have as much of the paint off as you can. Wait until you see the last traces of paint in the grain or other details swell, then use a brass-bristle brush to clean out the details.

workSmart

A dental pick or small finish nail can be used to pick paint out of areas where the brush can't reach.

Stripping carved and detailed pieces

This walnut table has a pierced fretwork edge and a highly carved pedestal base. I never use liquid refinishers on this type of furniture because of all the details. Paste-type methylene chloride strippers work best. A second choice would be an NMP stripper.

1. **Dismantle the piece** as much as possible. I took the top off the base. It's easier to strip the parts separately.

2. **Apply the stripper with a brush.** Use the brush to "poke" the stripper into the pierced edge.

3. **Remove the finish from the flat areas** using a putty knife.

4. **Apply planer chips to the details.** Then rub with a nylon brush to remove the finish.

5. **Use a round bristle brush** to push through the open areas of the fretwork. Brush up and down. Terry-cloth rags will also work for this purpose.

6. **Apply planer chips to the base** and use a nylon brush to remove the finish.

7. **For turned parts,** twine used shoe-shine style works the finish out of the deep recesses.

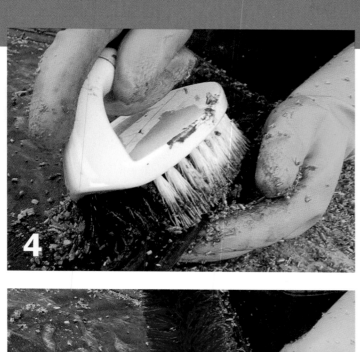

Surface preparation

Once the wood has been stripped, you'll need to prepare the surface to make sure the finish goes on properly and you get a good final surface. When furniture is manufactured, the main function of surface preparation is to remove the machining marks left after construction. When you refinish furniture, the removal of machining marks has been done. Even so, you'll need to sand the wood. Whether you do just a light sanding or sand more aggressively, this step ensures that the wood is clean and will stain and finish correctly. A more aggressive sanding may be necessary if you want to remove the inevitable marks of age, such as scratches and nicks.

In addition to sanding, you may need to address other blemishes. There may be gray or black water stains on the wood, or you may have some dents and gouges that need to be corrected. In this chapter, I show you how to prepare the wood after stripping and how to deal with surface repair issues particular to refinishing wood.

To see if the wood is ready for stain or a clear finish, wipe the surface with some solvent (mineral spirits, denatured alcohol, or lacquer thinner). This will highlight any dents, scratches, or areas that might need bleaching or other treatment.

Sanding

If the wood has a consistent color (with no areas of stains or grayish spots) after stripping and rinsing with solvent, all you need to do is sand. Whether you start with coarse papers or medium to fine papers depends on the quality of the surface. If there are dents and depressions, scratches or gouges, and you want to remove them, start sanding with a 100-grit or 120-grit sandpaper. If you have a fairly clean surface, or you want to leave the dents and scratches to preserve the old look of the piece, you can start with 150-grit or 180-grit sandpaper. If you have water spots, gray or black areas, or other discoloration, you will have to use wood bleach to remove them.

Most people sand too much (and with too fine a grit), or they don't level the wood well enough and miss areas. The technique I use alleviates both problems and can be used in both hand sanding and machine sanding.

Basic sanding techniques

Whether you sand by hand or machine, the goal is the same. You level the surface with coarse grits, then move on to finer grits to smooth the surface. A good place to start is with 100-grit paper if there are large scratches, dents, or other defects. Otherwise, you can start with 150 grit.

Choosing sandpaper products

Sandpaper products are available in a wide variety of shapes, styles, and forms, from flat sheets of paper to cushioned pads. Sandpaper sheets are the most common type of sandpaper and are designed for hand use and with quarter- or half-sheet electric sanders. Three types of sandpaper, designated by the type of abrasive, are used in refinishing:

• **Garnet**, a natural mineral, is used for hand-sanding applications and is available only in sheets.

• **Aluminum oxide**, a synthetic abrasive, is available in a wider variety of styles and is used for hand-sanding or machine sanding. It's tougher than garnet and lasts longer.

• **Silicon carbide** is the toughest grit used in sandpaper. The most common type used in refinishing work is the black or grayish colored wet-or-dry sandpaper that's used in between coats of finish and rubbing out the finish. It's used with a lubricant—typically water, but mineral spirits can also be used. Wet-or-dry sandpaper is never used on bare wood.

The gray areas and black marks on this oak table need a treatment of bleach. Sanding it first makes the bleach penetrate better.

The general idea is to work the surface with the sandpaper until the marks are removed and the surface is level. Then switch to a higher grit and sand until the previous (deeper) scratches are removed. If you have trouble seeing whether you removed the sanding scratches, use a light positioned directly behind the work area. (Or position your project so it gets backlighting from a window.) The final grit to which you should sand bare wood is 220. Wiping the surface with mineral spirits when you're finished will highlight any spots you missed. You can touch these up by returning to a lower grit and repeating the steps.

If the surface has damage, such as scratches or small gouges, level it first using 100 grit. Always sand in the grain direction of the wood. If you're sanding by hand, tear the sandpaper into quarters and wrap it around a cork, rubber, or soft wooden block. This levels the surface more efficiently than sanding with the grain. After several passes across the entire width, switch to the

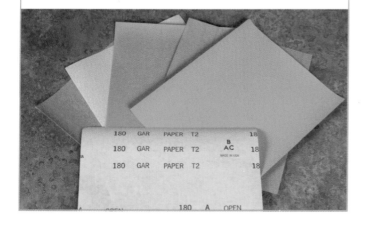

A sanding block makes the sandpaper cut faster and more evenly.

Sandpaper grits

CAMI	FEPA (P)*	Generic	Use for	Chapter
2000			Fine scratch removal and repairs	9
1500		Micro fine	Fine scratch removal and repairs	9
1200			Rubbing out a finish	8
1000			Rubbing out a finish	8
800	P2000	Ultra fine	Rubbing out a finish	8
	P1500		Rubbing out a finish	8
600	P1200		Rubbing out a finish	8
400	P800	Super fine	Sanding between coats	8
	P600		Sanding between coats	8
320	P400		Sanding between coats	8
	P320	Extra fine	Sanding sealer	8
220	P220		Sanding bare wood	6
180	P180		Sanding bare wood	6
150	P150	Fine	Sanding bare wood	6
120	P120		Sanding bare wood	6
100	P100	Medium	Sanding bare wood	6
80	P80	Coarse	Sanding bare wood	6

*This grade mark precedes the grit number on the sandpaper, for example, "P400."

As you sand, look at the surface lit from behind so you can make sure you're sanding evenly and removing the marks you want to remove.

workSmart

If the furniture is veneered, I suggest only hand-sanding with fine sandpaper (150 grit and higher). If you're not sure whether the furniture is veneered or solid wood, you can check the edges or the underside to see if the wood is a different color or grain pattern, which suggests it's veneered.

opposite direction (still with the grain) and repeat. Switch to the next grit (120) and sand with the grain until all the scratches from the previous grit are gone. Then go on up to 150, 180, and finally 220.

Some people say you should sand to a higher grit. In over 30 years of refinishing furniture, I have yet to see any advantage in sanding beyond 220 grit. Plus using high grits (400 and above) can actually impede the coloring action of some stains. I don't recommend it.

Surface repairs

Sanding may not remove all the defects from the surface. If the surface is otherwise in good shape except for a small dent or gouge and you don't want to sand the wood too aggressively, which would remove all the patina, you'll have to fill the defect or steam it out.

Dents can usually be swelled level with heat and water. Drop some distilled water into the dent and cover it with a wet cloth (use distilled water on the cloth, too). With a household iron set to just below high, place the tip of it on the cloth, over the dent for a few seconds. Remove it, and repeat the process until the dent comes up to the surface or at least close to it. When the

Dents like this can usually be swelled level with a little heat and water. It's much faster than sanding, which would remove too much wood.

Deep cracks in the wood should always be filled with wood putty.

surface has dried, a light sanding with 180 or 220 grit is all that's needed.

Use wood putty to fill cracks, splits, and gouges or dents that won't steam out. Putty is available in oil-based, water-based, and solvent-based forms. Water based is the easiest to use because it cleans up with water.

The trick with putty is to apply it to the defect only. If the putty gets into open pores on surrounding wood, it's hard to remove and will be visible once a finish is applied. To get around this problem, mask off the defect with masking tape before applying the putty. After the putty dries, sand it level.

Bleaching

If the wood appears too dark after stripping and some preliminary sanding, or you see a stubborn gray or black stain that doesn't come out, you'll need to use wood bleach.

The two most common bleaches used in refinishing are oxalic acid and chlorine bleach. A third type of bleach, called two-part, or A/B, bleach is also used, but rarely. The bleach most often used in refinishing is oxalic acid, which will remove gray and black water stains. It will lighten and even out tannin-rich woods like oak. You can find oxalic acid in most hardware and paint stores. Chlorine bleach can remove or lighten deep-penetrating dyes that remain after stripping. Chlorine bleach is available as liquid laundry bleach. Two-part bleach is used only to lighten the natural color of wood if it's too dark.

warning

Never put wood outside or in a hot area to force the bleach to dry faster or the wood will warp.

Oxalic acid (far left) is often available in hardware stores. The Two-part wood bleach (right, front) may be hard to find locally and you may have to order it from a finishing supplier. Super-strength chlorine bleach (shock treatment) is available at pool-supply stores. The main ingredient is calcium hypochlorite (left, front).

Choosing a bleach

Desired action	Bleach to use	Neutralize with
Lighten the natural color of wood	A/B (two-part) bleach	2 parts water, 1 part white vinegar
Remove dye stains	Chlorine bleach	2 to 3 applications of distilled water
Remove iron stains	Oxalic acid	3 applications of distilled water
Lighten stripped wood	Oxalic acid	3 applications of distilled water
Remove water stains	Oxalic acid	3 applications of distilled water

If a stain is unknown, try oxalic acid first, then chlorine bleach second. Always rinse the first bleach off completely with distilled water before applying a second.

Oxalic acid is available as a dry powder or crystals. The powder is mixed with hot water until no more dissolves. Typically the ratio is 3 oz. by weight to 1 qt. hot water. Apply the bleach to the entire wood surface, not just the stain. It may take several applications, with several hours' drying time in between, to get the stain out. After drying, rinse the wood three times with distilled water to remove all traces of the bleach.

Chlorine bleach is used to remove residual dye stains and some other stains on bare wood like grape juice and tea that don't come out with oxalic acid. The bleaching agent in household bleach is dilute sodium hypochlorite. Buy it fresh because bleaches lose their strength if they have been sitting around for more than a few months.

Apply the bleach and let it sit overnight. Several applications may be necessary if the stain doesn't come out completely. If the stain doesn't come out after several applications, you can try a more concentrated form of chlorine bleach which is sold as "shock treatment" for swimming pools (calcium hypochlorite). Mix 1 tablespoon of the dry powder with 1 cup hot water for very strong chlorine bleach. After the wood is dry, apply a solution of 1 part white vinegar and 2 parts water.

Two-part bleach is the least-used bleach, but it will remove the natural color of some dark woods. For example, if you have an old dresser made from dark oak or birch that you want to lighten up, use A/B bleach. The downside of this type of bleach is that it's hard to find locally, but it can be ordered from woodworking or refinishing suppliers.

Final steps

Once surface preparation is complete, start applying your finishes within 24 hours if possible. Furniture parts left propped up against walls or lying around will invariably get dirty or, worse, get dented from a fall. After the final sanding, wipe the wood with denatured alcohol to remove sanding debris dust and other particles before applying stains or other finishing products.

After you've completed your sanding and other surface preparation, a quick wipe down with a non-grain-raising solvent like denatured alcohol will remove sanding debris and leave a clean surface for stains or other finishing products.

Sanding by hand

Determine in advance whether you want to leave the signs of wear and tear on a piece. This collectible Mission rocker shouldn't be sanded too aggressively or the original color will be removed. In this case, we're not using a sanding block or starting with a lower-grit sandpaper so that we can preserve the original patina.

1. **Tear a sheet of 180-grit** sandpaper into quarters. Tearing against a table edge gives a cleaner cut.

2. **Fold a quartered sheet** into thirds by folding the sandpaper over itself to make a pad.

3. **Sand the surface with the grain** using your hand (not a sanding block).

4. **Keep the sandpaper flat** when sanding edges and try not to hold it so it cuts through any sharp edges.

5. **Sand round or nonflat parts** like this turned leg with foam sanding pads so you don't cut through edges.

6. **Use small pieces of sandpaper** for hand-sanding complex edges or other details.

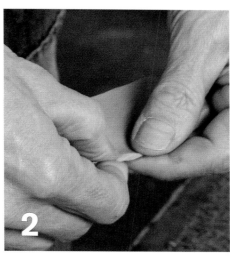

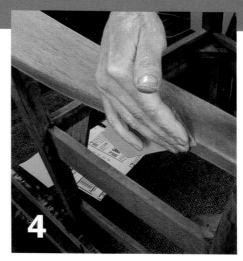

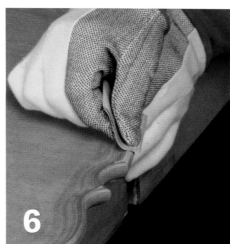

Sanding to remove flaws

This oak top had a lot of small dents and scratches as well as black marks from water. I began with coarse sandpaper to remove the imperfections and to prepare for bleaching. Sanding ensures that the bleach will penetrate.

1. **Use 100-grit sandpaper** mounted on a power sander or a sanding block. Sand in the direction of the grain.

2. **Check periodically** to see if you're removing the flaws by backlighting the work area and getting your eye at the level of the surface.

3. **Use a power sander** for deep scratches or dents like those shown.

4. **Move the sander** in the direction of the grain to achieve an even effect. After using the 100-grit sandpaper, I bleached out the stains and allowed the wood to dry thoroughly. Then I continued to sand using 120, 150, 180, and then 220 grit.

workSmart

If I'm using an electric sander, I like to hand-sand after I'm done with 220 grit with the grain to make sure there are no electric sander swirls in the final surface.

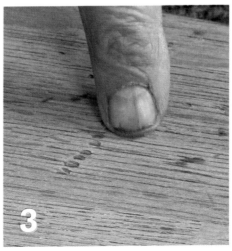

Steaming out a dent

Dents that are too large and deep to sand out can usually be steamed level with the surface using a household iron and distilled water. My rule of thumb is that any dent larger than a pencil eraser should be steamed out.

1. **Pour a little puddle** of distilled water into the dent.

2. **Put a piece of cotton cloth dampened with distilled** water over the dent. Set a household iron to "cotton" (usually one or two steps below the highest setting). Place the iron over the rag and hold it for about 15 seconds.

3. **Repeat Steps 2 and 3.** Several (three to four) applications of heat should swell the dent close to the surface. It's OK if you don't make it perfect.

4. **Sand the entire surface** with 100-grit sandpaper to make the dent disappear completely.

Using wood putty

Sanding will never fix this stress crack, which goes all the way through this oak top. Wood putty is the only fix. When using putty on an open-grained wood like oak, it's important to isolate the putty. Otherwise, it gets into the grain and will be visible after applying finishes and stains.

1. **Use blue painter's tape** to mask the area around the cracks (or dents if applicable).

2. **Apply the putty** with your fingers, pushing it down into the crack. You can also use a putty knife to work it into the crack and remove excess putty.

3. **Let the putty dry.** Follow the manufacturer's directions. This water-based putty was ready to go in 4 hours. Remove the tape.

4. **Sand level with a sanding block** mounted with 150-grit or 180-grit sandpaper. The tape has the added benefit of leaving the putty raised a little above the wood, making it easier to sand level.

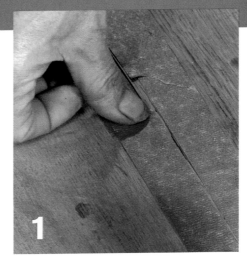

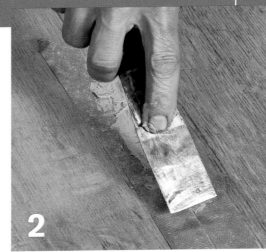

Using oxalic acid wood bleach

or oxalic acid bleach to work effectively, sand the surface first so that the bleach can penetrate. Sand with the grit appropriate for the stage of sanding—100 grit if you're level sanding, 150 grit to 180 grit if you're not trying to remove imperfections. Don't apply more than two applications of bleach because it won't be effective.

1. **Mix the dry powder** with hot water until no more powder will dissolve. Typically, the ratio is 3 oz. to 1 qt. water. (Follow the manufacturer's recommendations.)

2. **Apply the bleach to the entire surface,** not just the stains. Spread the bleach liberally with a rag or sponge.

3. **Allow the bleach to work.** The black areas disappear almost immediately but wait until the wood is dry. If you see a faint outline of a black stain still visible, apply bleach as you did in Step 2.

4. **Allow the final application of bleach to dry overnight.** Typically the marks are bleached enough so they won't be too visible under a finish. Rinse the wood three times with distilled water to remove all traces of the bleach.

Staining and grain filling

Grain filler is a product designed to give open-pored woods like this mahogany table a glass-smooth finish.

I f you're satisfied with the color and texture of the wood after stripping the finish and sanding, just proceed to applying a clear finish. Keep in mind that applying a clear finish will darken the color a bit, which you can check beforehand by wiping the surface with mineral spirits. If you had a different look in mind for your project, you have options for changing it.

Do you want to change the color? If you'd prefer a different color, you can apply a stain to the wood. Stains are transparent colorants that allow the grain and figure of the wood to show through. Do you like the look of open-pored woods such as oak, walnut, and mahogany? If not, you can smooth the surface with grain filler. In this chapter, I discuss stains and grain fillers and how to use them.

Grain fillers

All woods have vessels that conduct sap to the leaves when the tree is alive. When the tree is cut into lumber, these vessels are sliced open, revealing channels in the wood that look like straws cut open lengthwise. These are called *pores*. When the pores on hardwoods are visible to the naked eye we call the wood open-pored. Some woods, such as oak and ash, have very large pores, which

give the wood a discernible rough texture when you touch it. On other hardwoods like mahogany and walnut the pores are smaller and less obvious to the touch, but they are visible once finish is applied. Hardwoods, such as maple, cherry, and birch, and softwoods, such as pine, have pores so small that they are filled with the finishes applied to them and aren't visible.

You can leave the pores open. Open-pored finishes have a more natural, less-sophisticated look that many woodworkers prefer. Filling the grain is an extra step and takes time. If you want a glass-smooth, refined finished surface on open-pored woods (called a filled-pored finish), use grain filler, also known as "paste wood filler." Some examples of filled-pored finishes are elegant dining tables and musical instruments with glossy, mirror-like finishes.

The oak plant stand (top) has a more natural and less-refined look because the distinctive oak grain is visible. The mahogany tabletop (bottom) has a glass-smooth, mirror-like surface appropriate to its Federal style.

The water-based grain filler (left) is ready to use right out of the can. The thicker, dual-purpose wood and crack filler (right) should be thinned with a little water when used for filling grain.

A rubber squeegee designed for paste filler application is very helpful and the corner can be used to remove filler from corners and crevices.

The oil based filler I'm using here is colored dark so it highlights the grain as well as fills it.

Oil-based vs. water-based grain fillers

Grain fillers are seldom available at hardware stores, paint stores, or home centers. Order them from online woodworking or finishing retailers. Oil-based grain filler is becoming more difficult to find because of environmental regulations. It can also pose adhesion issues with water-based clear finishes, but it should work fine under oil-based top-coat finishes.

The main advantage of water-based filler is that any stain or finish can be applied over it. Water-based grain fillers are sold as ready-to-use products or dual-purpose grain and crack filler products. Because the components of grain filler and putties and fillers used for filling gouges and dents are the same, you can use them for grain filling after thinning with water.

Tools for grain filling

You don't need sophisticated tools for applying grain filler. A brush or a piece of coarse cloth will work fine. You could use a rubber squeegee sold specifically for applying grain filler. This specialized tool packs the filler down into the pores and removes excess from the surface at the same time. Or you could use an old credit card or a stiff piece of cardboard. Also have some rags and sandpaper on hand to remove the excess filler from the dried surface.

Using grain filler

We'll focus on water-based filler because it can be used under any finish and is easy to find. Use water-based fillers after sanding and before staining because they will allow a stain to penetrate once they dry. Pick a color that complements the wood's natural color if you intend to leave it unstained. Choose a darker color if you plan to stain it after the grain filler or if you want the grain to stand out. Apply the grain filler with a brush, remove the excess with a rubber squeegee or a piece of cardboard, and then let it dry.

Use 220-grit sandpaper to sand the excess filler until the wood surface is clean but the pores remain filled. Let the filler dry for at least 24 hours before finishing. While the surface may look chalky at first, this haze disappears as soon as you apply finish or stain.

The most common type of stain you'll find locally is called wiping stain (left). Gel stains (right) are thicker and won't drip or run.

Stains

Stains are liquids that color wood but still allow the grain and figure to show. The most common type is an oil- or water- based pigment stain called a *wiping stain.* These products are easy to use. They work well on open-grained woods like oak, mahogany, and walnut. However, if you want to achieve a very dark color on hard, close-grained woods like maple, you'll need to use a dye stain.

Dyes are available as premixed liquids, powders, or concentrates. They are seldom sold in hardware stores or home centers but can be purchased from online finish suppliers or specialty woodworking retailers. Dye stains are usually indicated as such on the label or are sold bottled and ready to use as NGR (non-grain-raising) stains. If the container does not specifically say *dye* somewhere, it's probably a pigment stain or pigment–dye combination. In either case, application is similar.

Using stains

Check the instructions on the can and stir the contents if indicated. Using a brush or rag, apply the stain quickly over the entire surface and then wipe excess off with a clean rag. The amount of open time (the time you have before the stain starts to dry) you have to work the stain is important. Oil-based products evaporate more slowly

Dye stains are available as ready to go premixed products (right) or concentrated powders and liquids (left). They can be purchased from woodworking stores or online retailers.

A water-free, non-grain-raising stain is called an **NGR** stain. This type is always dye based and dries very quickly.

The left side of this mix of different woods was treated with a stain controller. While effective most of the time, you can see on one of the woods it didn't help. Blotching like this can be fixed by scrubbing the stain off with lacquer thinner and steel wool after it's dried.

Double-staining means applying the same stain after the first one has dried. In this case, it was used to make the outside wood on this door panel match the darker color of the inside panel.

than water-based products and allow you plenty of time to apply and then wipe off the stain evenly. That's why oil-based stains are the most popular. Make sure the wood is free of sanding debris before you apply them.

Stain problems

The number one problem with staining is a condition known as blotching. Certain woods, notably softwoods like pine and some hardwoods like cherry, poplar, and soft maple, will stain unevenly due to variations in density at the wood surface.

The best method to control blotching is to use a wash coat or stain controller (widely available and also known as wood conditioner) before applying the stain. The liquid is absorbed into the surface and seals the wood, preventing the stain from penetrating unevenly.

Match the type of controller to the stain you're using. Use an oil-based controller with oil-based stains; water-based controllers work for water-based stains. Alternatively, you can use a thin coat of finish, shellac, lacquer, or varnish (called a *wash coat*) for just about any stain. I cut the finish 50:50 with its thinner to use as a stain controller. Thinned shellac is my favorite; it dries in about an hour and works with nearly any stain, except those that are alcohol based. For these stains, use an oil-based stain controller.

Restaining and glazes

Once your project has been stained, you may find that some parts (such as the top and base) don't match. You can stain again to equalize a section that's lighter, but do it only after the first stain has fully dried and don't apply more than one more coat of stain. You can also apply color after the first coat of finish. This technique is known as glazing.

Glazing can be used to match woods of different species. Some manufactured furniture may have nice wood on visible surfaces such as tops and fronts, but the legs, stretchers, or other surfaces may be a less expensive wood such as poplar or gum. After the piece is stripped and stained and you start applying finish you may find that some parts don't match. In this case, you can apply a glaze over the partially sealed surface and alter the color. Another use for glazes is to subtly correct or enhance the overall color (see "Layering color to match" on p. 92).

Glazes can be found at specialty woodworking stores, good paint stores, or online. If you have trouble finding glaze, you can use a pigment gel stain. These are sold only in oil-based versions. If you want an all water-based finish, you need to find a water-based glaze or use a water-based pigment stain.

Fine-tuning the stain color

The goal of staining is to produce an even color that's the color you want. As long as the stain has not dried, you have several options for adjusting the color.

To lighten the stain, apply the solvent for the stain before it cures. If the color is still too dark, scrub the area with some fine synthetic steel wool moistened with the solvent that thins or cleans up the stain.

To darken a stain, use a darker colored stain. Letting the stain dry longer in the hopes of making the stain darker doesn't work. The best strategy is to apply the stain and then immediately wipe off the excess. If you're using a dye that you mixed, make a stronger dye solution by adding more dye. If using a wiping stain, allow the first coat of stain to dry, then apply another.

To change the color, apply a different colored stain while the first stain is still wet.

If a rag doesn't remove enough stain, try using a gray synthetic abrasive pad dampened with solvent.

To darken a light stain, restain it after the first stain has dried or apply a glaze.

Using a glaze

To glaze over something that's been stained and has a coat of finish or sealer applied, sand the dried finish with a piece of gray synthetic steel wool to smooth it slightly. Apply the glaze and wipe the excess off just as you would a stain. The nice thing about a glaze is that if you don't like the color or effect, you can wipe it all off using the cleanup solvent for the glaze or stain.

A particularly nice effect with glaze for old furniture is to selectively apply a dark glaze or stain to recessed areas, corners, and crevices with a small brush to imitate the build up of dirt and wax that you would typically see on antique furniture.

A dark stain-glaze was applied to this pine door after one coat of lighter stain. The lighter stain was sealed with one coat of finish. The dark stain remains in the age marks and crevices, giving the door a pleasing antique look.

Manufacturers' samples are helpful to match finish colors, but don't rely on them alone. Avoid matching sample woods with completely different grain patterns, such as oak to a pine finish.

Store sample boards are always on pine and oak. When you have cherry to match (a darker wood) you might have to buy stains a shade lighter to compensate.

Matching color

When you refinish furniture, you may want the finished piece to match or, at least, blend in with the other furniture in your room. Or you might have to make a new piece of wood for a damaged part on an antique and match it to the old wood's color.

Matching a finished stain color exactly is challenging even for pros because there are so many variables: the texture and color of the wood, the sheen of the finish, and the vibrancy of the color. The original finish could be an intense color or subdued and muted. Many external

If you're using the same species of wood in your match (in this case cherry), many times you may find a color for a near perfect match.

factors affect how we perceive color, even the lighting in the room.

You can approach matching a color in one of two ways: match a color to a sample board or layer colors until you achieve the color you want. The second method gives you the most control, particularly if you're trying to match a factory finish or you're unsure of the products used in the original finish.

Mixing to match

At its simplest, matching a stain involves finding the right single stain for the job. If you already own stains that may work, test them on a piece of scrap of the same species as your project. Otherwise, compare store samples of actual stained wood against the project—perhaps a door or drawer front you've removed for that purpose. If you're lucky, you'll find a perfect match. More likely, you'll find a stain color "between" two colors, perhaps a bit lighter or darker. If the store sells small cans of the stain (half pints or less), you can purchase several colors.

Experiment with the stain or stains on scraps of wood of the same species as your project. If the color is too dark, try diluting it a bit with the cleanup solvent for the stain. If it's not quite the color you want, you can often "push" it toward a slightly different hue (red or yellow or orange) by wiping it with a different color stain while both colors are still wet.

Try to approximate the lightest color in the wood you're trying to match. When you've got an idea of the proper colors to use and whether they need dilution, mix up a small amount of liquid to test, noting the approximate proportions of the mixture. Test it on your scrap again and make any necessary adjustments to the mixture, again noting the proportions.

Water-soluble dye stains made from powders or concentrates are easy to adjust by adding more dye (making it darker) or adding more water (making it lighter).

Here's a trick to avoid applying the wrong color to your actual project. Before applying wiping stain, wipe the stain on a piece of glass or clear acrylic, then place the glass over the first stain to get an idea of the final color.

Layering color

Another approach and the one many professionals use is to apply colors in layers, building up to the desired final color. This method gives you the most control, particularly if you're trying to match a dark finish.

The easiest layering technique is to apply a wiping stain over a dye, which allows you to sneak up on the final color. If you don't have any samples of scrap wood to practice on, you can always use the nonshow side of a part from your project (the underside of a top or the rear of a drawer front).

Begin by applying a dye stain that approximates the hue of the final color but is a bit lighter. I like using water-soluble dye powders or concentrates that are reduced with water. This way I can dial in the desired lighter base color. Get close to the color you're trying to match but leave it lighter. You'll finalize the color in the next step.

Seal the stain before applying a wiping stain that matches the desired final color. I use dewaxed shellac for this step, primarily because it dries fast. Let the shellac dry at least several hours and then sand it lightly with 320-grit sandpaper. Remove the sanding dust with a tack rag. Experiment with different colors of wiping stain until you get the look that you want. The beauty of this technique is that the sealer allows an errant color stain to be easily wiped away for a second (or third) try.

Lighting for matching colors

When you match a finish, it's best to work in diffused (not direct) natural daylight from windows or under special fluorescent bulbs that are daylight balanced and have a CRI (color rendering index) above 90. Never try and match a color using standard fluorescent bulbs designated cool white or incandescent light bulbs. The two fluorescent bulbs shown below are examples of daylight balanced. In the long numbers on the bulbs, the most important are the *C50* at the end. Or look for the term *5000K* in the product description, which means a color temperature of 5000 Kelvin.

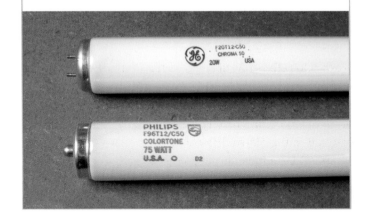

Using a water-based grain filler

This mahogany tabletop is a good candidate for grain filler because of its classic, refined design. I picked a water-based filler that complements the natural color of the wood.

1. **Use a small cotton rag** to apply the filler to just the flat areas (the carved edges don't need it).

2. **Use a rubber squeegee** sold for grain filler to remove as much of the excess filler as you can. (You can also use a piece of stiff cardboard or an old credit card.) Don't worry if you can't remove it all. All the excess will be removed by sanding in the next step.

3. **Allow the filler to dry** at least 4 hours or the time recommended by the manufacturer. When it's dry, sand with 220-grit sandpaper wrapped around a sanding block.

4. **Vacuum off the dust** and examine the surface for excess filler by wiping it with a rag dampened with water. Excess filler can be removed by adding a little denatured alcohol to the water and wiping with the rag.

Using an oil-based grain filler

Oil-based filler is applied in a similar manner as water-based filler except it works best when used over a sealed surface. One application of a 2-lb. cut dewaxed shellac product works best. With oil-based filler, stain the wood first, then apply the shellac sealer.

1. **Apply the filler** over a stained and shellac-sealed surface with a cheap bristle brush.

2. **Remove the excess filler** with a squeegee. A piece of cardboard or a credit card can be used in a pinch.

3. **Let the filler sit until it hazes** (usually 15 minutes to 20 minutes), then remove the excess with a coarse cloth like burlap.

4. **Use small pieces of wood** to remove filler from detailed areas or corners. If you want to put a water-based finish over an oil-based grain filler, apply a sealer coat of dewaxed shellac.

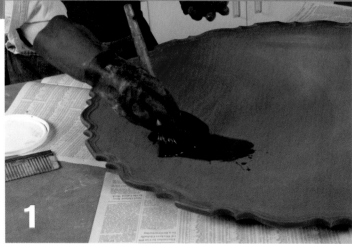

Applying a wiping stain

Use color samples provided by the stain manufacturer to determine the right color for your project. If you can test the stain on a hidden area such as the underside of a top, you'll avoid potential problems when you work on the show surfaces.

1. **Apply the stain** with a bristle brush, working it into the grain really well if it's an open-grained wood by brushing back and forth against the grain.

2. **Take a clean rag** and wipe off the excess stain, turning the rag frequently to expose fresh, clean cloth.

3. **Use a piece of the cloth** to remove the stain from corners and details or a dry, clean brush in a whisking motion.

4. **Take a few final passes with a clean cloth,** going in the direction of the grain to remove any rag smudges.

Applying a dye stain

Water-based dye stains are a good choice when you want really dark colors. Dye stains dry fast, so it's important to assemble all the supplies you need beforehand so you have immediate access to them.

1. **Use a sponge to saturate the surface** with the dye. Wipe it on quickly, keeping the dye wet over the entire surface you're working. Note that I took the base off this old coat rack to dye separately.

2. **Wipe off the excess dye** with a clean cloth.

3. **Use a plant mister** for complicated areas like the base. These inexpensive spray bottles make a great applicator for the dye stains.

4. **When the dye has dried,** the wood will look dry and chalky. If the wood grain is rough after drying, you can smooth it with some synthetic steel wool.

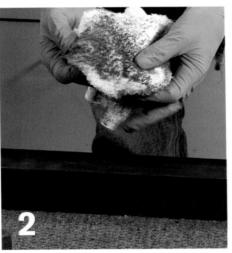

Using a stain controller

S tain controllers are sold in water-based and oil-based versions. Make sure you match the stain controller to the type of stain you're using. This sequence shows the effect of conditioner on several wood species to demonstrate which blotch under stain and which don't.

1. **Apply the conditioner** liberally to the surface using a brush or rag. Allow it to penetrate for 30 minutes.

2. **Apply the stain.** (In this case, I'm using an oil-based stain.)

3. **Allow the stain to dry.** Note that almost all the wood samples that had the conditioner applied (left side) look good, except the maple, which is the second one from the bottom.

workSmart

Even after taking precautions with stain controllers, a wood may still splotch. If this happens, let the wood dry and then scrub off as much of the stain as you can with steel wool and lacquer thinner. Reapplying furniture stripper and sanding with 100-grit sandpaper will also work.

Glazing basics

This mahogany table shows a common problem in refinishing. The highly figured mahogany-veneered top has become much darker than the solid wood base after one coat of finish was applied. This is a job solved by glazing.

1. **Scuff the finish lightly** using very fine (maroon) synthetic steel wool.

2. **A gel stain** makes a great glaze in a pinch. This Georgian cherry color is a different color from the original stain but that doesn't matter. We just want to darken the color a bit.

3. **Apply the glaze with a brush** over a manageable area.

4. **Wipe off the excess stain with a cloth.** Don't let the stain remain too long or it will become tacky and difficult to remove. Notice how the extra bit of color gives more depth to the base.

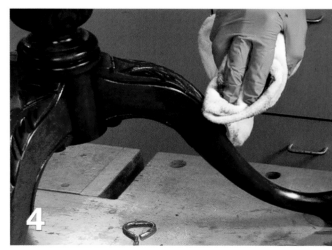

Matching color using sample boards

Most sample boards are made from pine and oak. If you have another species in your project, you may have to purchase several different colors to compensate. In this project, we're also matching two kinds of wood: a mahogany top to a cherry drawer front.

1. **Compare colors in natural daylight,** if possible, not artificial indoor lighting, which throws off the colors.

2. **Pick the color that matches best,** noting the different effects that the samples have on the pine and oak. If the store sells stains in small cans, buy a couple of lighter and darker shades as well.

3. **Use a scrap of the same species** as in your project for the sample board. In this case, I used a piece of mahogany that was similar to the antique tabletop I was trying to match to the drawer front.

4. **Apply the stains you purchased to your sample.** Here, one of the stains matches closely.

5. **Apply the best-matching stain to your project.**

6. **Compare the color match to the finished piece** you're trying to match. When I held the drawer to the top, the top definitely looked darker than the sample piece.

7. **To lighten the stain,** wipe down the part with solvent before it dries. To deepen the color, remove the excess from the first coat with a clean cloth, then apply another coat of stain after the first coat dries. Or apply a darker stain over the first stain.

4

7

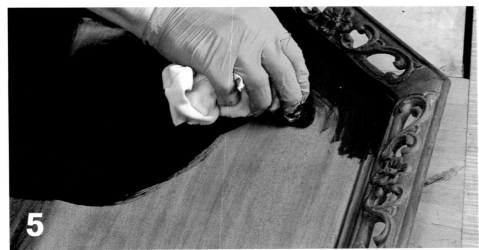

5

◖workSmart

Make sure you determine the match while the stain is wet because the color shifts as it soaks into the wood and dries.

6

Layering color to match

The top to this very old solid cherry table was too damaged to save, so I made a new top. I have to match the new top to the old cherry color. I'm looking to blend the new with the old, for a pleasing overall effect.

1. **Wipe the wood with solvent** (mineral spirits) to see how far off the color is. Note that the grain direction determines the depth of the color, which is why the side looks lighter in the photo.

2. **Pick from the manufacturer's sample chart** to find the best-matching water-soluble dye. Mix a small amount and test on a sample board. In this case, it was way too dark.

3. **Dilute the mixed stain 1:1 with water** and try again. If it's still too dark, keep diluting with water, noting how much water you added each time, until you get a close match that's lighter than the desired final color. It's important that it be lighter because you'll darken it with the next steps.

4. **Seal the surface with a coat of dewaxed shellac sealer.** Sometimes the shellac will darken the color just enough to match. If it's not dark enough, you can darken it in the next step. Let it dry for 2 hours and then sand with 320 grit.

5. **Test an assortment of pigment stains** until you find one that is a match. Apply the best-matching pigment stain.

6. **Apply a top-coat finish** after the stain dries. I applied three coats of lacquer to the whole piece and then rubbed it down to a satin finish. The photo shows the table with the new top compared to the drawer used for matching.

Applying a finish

A clear finish provides protection from spills, dents, and scrapes. It also creates a clear lens that lets the figure and beauty of the wood show through.

There are many choices for wood finishes, but the most useful for refinishers are oil finishes, shellac, polyurethane, and lacquer. Polyurethane and lacquer are now available in water-based versions, which are a good choice because they are non-flammable and have a low odor. Most of these finishes, both oil based and water based, are available at better hardware and paint stores as well as most home centers. The main differences among these finishes are the degree of protection they offer, how easy they are to apply, and how fast they dry. In this chapter, I explain how to choose a finish and show you the basics of finish application.

Choosing a finish

There are many brands and types of finishes. Some require skill to apply or are hard to find. These are best left to pros with the right equipment, finishing environment, and expertise to apply them. The finishes we'll look at

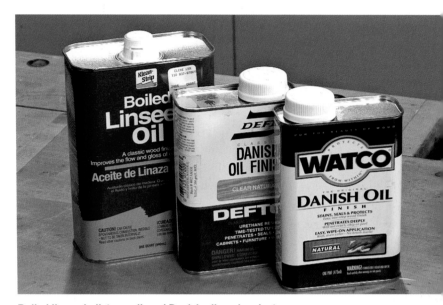

Boiled linseed oil, tung oil, and Danish oil are low-luster, natural looking finishes for wood that accentuate grain and figure but aren't very durable.

here are easy to find and can be applied successfully by most weekend refinishers.

Pure and penetrating oils

Pure and penetrating oils are available as boiled linseed oil, tung oil, and Danish oil. They are the easiest finish to apply and look best on projects that won't get harsh abuse, such as clocks, radio cases, plate racks, and display pieces. Pure oils such as boiled linseed and tung oil are used as a nontoxic, safe finish for toys and food-preparation items. These finishes come from natural products and dry in the wood, not on top where they would peel or crack. The main disadvantage of these finishes is that they don't offer much physical protection because they lie in the wood, not on top.

warning

When working with oil-based finishes, especially pure and penetrating oils, be careful to dispose of the rags properly as they can pose a risk of fire.

Oil-based wiping varnishes and polyurethanes are easy to apply and offer more protection than pure oil finishes like tung and boiled linseed oil.

Lacquer finishes dry quickly, and most are plenty durable for furniture finishes.

When shellac is used under another finish as a sealer, you should always use dewaxed shellac (right). Aerosol shellac is very handy for finishing small projects. The shellac-containing wax (left) is available as orange or clear (actually a pale amber).

Oil-based varnish and polyurethane

Oil-based finishes are the best all-around finishes. They are easy to apply, look as good as the pure and penetrating oil finishes, and offer more protection. My favorites are the wiping varnishes and polyurethanes because they are so easy to apply. If you want a subdued, antique look to your furniture, choose a satin finish. Or you can rub a gloss finish down to a satin sheen.

Shellac

Shellac is a favorite finish for refinishing antiques because most furniture made before 1940 used shellac as the finish. Shellac imparts a warm amber tone, doesn't have harsh fumes, dries fast, and doesn't react adversely to residual polishes and other contaminants that stripping and sanding don't adequately remove from the wood (see "Finishing problems" on p. 98). Shellac can be a little tricky to apply because it dries so fast and the only sheen available is gloss, so if you want a satin finish you'll have to rub it down (see "Rubbing a finish to satin" on p. 108).

Shellac is sold premixed or as raw flakes available from specialty woodworking stores. The flakes are dissolved in denatured alcohol to make a finish. There are more grades and colors available in flakes than in the premixed versions, and mixing shellac yourself guarantees a fresher finish. Premixed shellac is fine for most refinishing projects, but if you're using shellac as a sealer under another finish, it's important to use dewaxed shellac.

Lacquer

Lacquer is available in both water-based and solvent-based forms. It dries fast and is a good choice when you want a finish that can be rubbed to a high gloss. Solvent-based lacquer is arguably one of the best looking finishes but is tricky to apply with a brush. Unless you have spray equipment and have some experience spraying, choose water-based lacquer. It's easier to apply with a brush, has exceptional clarity, and is low odor. Water-based lacquer is a good choice if you have to work indoors and fumes and flammability are an issue.

(Left to right) Synthetic-bristle brushes are used for all water-based products and thin solvent-based finishes like shellac. Natural bristle brushes are for solvent-based finishes like polyurethane and varnish. Inexpensive, China-bristle brushes are for applying stains and other noncritical tasks.

Applying finishes

Oils and wiping varnishes are typically applied with rags or paper towels, while polyurethanes, shellac, and lacquer are applied with a brush.

Wiping on a finish

Wiping varnish and polyurethane and pure oil finishes like linseed, Danish, and tung oil can be wiped on with a rag. Pure oil finishes are the easiest finishes to apply because the finish is simply applied to the wood, allowed to sit for 5 minutes to 10 minutes, then wiped off. Wiping varnishes are a little harder to apply, but because they dry harder than oil, they provide more protection. I recommend them for novice refinishers because they dry more slowly and can be applied more evenly. Also, they don't raise the wood grain like water-based finishes.

To apply pure oil finishes, use an absorbent cloth or paper towel. Nontextured paper towels work very well. For film finishes, such as wiping varnish or polyurethane, the cloth should be as lint free as possible. Old cotton T-shirts are ideal.

Brushing a finish

Brushes are best for projects with a lot of detail like carvings and recesses because the bristles get into tight areas. Match the size of the brush to your project. Use 2-in. to 3-in. sizes for larger flat surfaces and smaller 1-in. to 1½-in. sizes for smaller projects or those with a lot of detail.

A 1½-in. chisel-edge brush is a great tool to get into the tight turned recesses on this antique table.

Brushes are divided into two groups—natural and synthetic. Natural-bristle brushes are commonly made from Chinese hogs (China bristle). Use natural-bristle brushes for solvent-based finishes (varnish, oil-based polyurethane, and lacquer) and shellac.

Synthetic bristle is made from man-made fibers like nylon and polyester. Always use synthetic-bristle brushes for applying water-based products, but you can also use synthetic-bristle brushes to apply most types of finishes.

It's a good idea to have at least one of each type (natural bristle and synthetic), and expect to pay at least $12 to $15 for good brushes and up to $30 for the best.

When using a brush never dip it into the finish past the metal ferrule, and with oil-based varnishes and oil-based varnishes and polyurethanes don't scrape the excess finish off on the lip of the container or you'll

Finishing problems

Two problems that often come up during refinishing are fisheye and drips and bubbles.

After wood is stripped, waxes and silicone from polishes can remain in the wood. Craters called *fisheyes* form in the finish (not shellac) as it comes in contact with the oils. Don't try to fix fisheye by trying to brush or wipe it away. Instead, remove the finish you just applied and go through the cleaning sequence explained in "Removing fisheye" on p. 104.

Bubbles occur with varnish and polyurethane and with some water-based products but not at all with shellac and lacquer or oils. Bubbles often result from using the wrong brush or too thick a finish. Try thinning the finish first, just an ounce or two per pint of finish to start. If that doesn't work, try switching to a different brush. Drips are easy to fix. Wipe them immediately and rebrush the area. If you miss a drip and it's partially dry, leave it alone; when it's dry, slice it off with a razor blade or sharp chisel.

Fisheye is the term for a refinishing problem where the newly applied finish crawls into ridges, forming little eyes.

If you don't catch a drip and it dries, the best way to level it is with a razor blade.

incorporate bubbles into the finish. When you're done using a brush,clean it by brushing the excess finish out on some newspaper, and then wash it vigorously in dishwashing deter-gent and water. When the bristles feel squeaky clean, wrap the brush in some paper towel to hold the shape and store it upright.

workSmart

If you are going to brush later in the day, you can wrap a brush in plastic food wrap or a rag to keep it from drying out.

To clean a brush first wipe the finish off. Then swirl it in cleanup solvent. Finally, rinse it with water and dishwashing detergent.

Traditional materials for hand-rubbing a finish include fine-grit abrasive sheets, steel wool pads, and polishing pastes and powders. Rottenstone and tripoli (rear) are available from woodworking suppliers.

Sanding between coats

Sanding between coats is necessary to remove minor imperfections like dust that may develop in the finish as it dries. Use a 320-grit or 400-grit paper. Sand lightly to shear off dust nibs and to slightly roughen the surface so the next coat will adhere.

Remove the dust with a tack cloth. Most tack cloths can leave a residue that causes problems with water-based finishes, so when using water-based products use a cloth dampened with water instead. With lacquer, shellac, and some water-based finishes, sanding between coats is necessary only to remove dust nibs or other glaring problems so you can safely apply two to three coats before sanding.

Rubbing out a finish

Rubbing out works best with hard, film-forming finishes like lacquer, shellac, varnishes, and polyurethanes. Don't expect results on thin, in-the-wood finishes like pure linseed or tung oil.

Materials for rubbing out

The basic concept of rubbing out a finish is simple—flatten the surface with fine sandpaper to remove surface defects and level it out. Then bring the finish to the desired sheen by polishing it. You can do this by hand, using traditional materials.

Fine-grit abrasive paper removes imperfections and levels the finish. A 600-grit sandpaper is available as wet-or-dry sandpaper, which is used with a liquid lubricant (called wet sanding) or as dry sanding sheets (generically called stearated sandpaper). Dry sandpapers tend to "corn up" with solvent lacquers, shellac, and varnishes, so I usually use wet-or-dry sandpaper. Soapy water (a capful of a dishwashing soap to a pint of water) makes a great lubricant.

If the finish powders when you sand it, it's dry enough to rub out.

The most widely available polishing products are 4F pumice and rottenstone. Rottenstone is finer than pumice. Use these products with paraffin oil or mineral oil.

Wax applied with 0000 steel wood results in a pleasing semigloss finish that's silky to the touch.

Steel-wool and abrasive pads aid in smoothing. Synthetic steel wool is known by trade names such as Scotch-Brite, Mirlon®, and Bear-Tex® and the grading is done by color. Gray is ultra fine and maroon is very fine. Regular steel wool is sold in the aught numbering system, the finest being 0000. For final smoothing, rubbing to a satin finish, and applying wax, use 0000 or (4-aught) steel wool. If you're using synthetic steel wool, choose the gray pads, or ultra fine.

Abrasive powders and pastes are used after smoothing with flat abrasives to polish the finish to the desired sheen. The traditional powder products for this step are 4F pumice and rottenstone, available from woodworking suppliers. These products are never used in dry form. You mix them with rubbing oil (also known as paraffin oil or light mineral oil).

If you can't find pumice and rottenstone or you want to save yourself some elbow grease, you can substitute automotive compounding product for 4F pumice and a final polish for the rottenstone. Sometimes these are just sold as two-step systems. You can use these products by hand or with round pads on an electric sander or polisher.

Sanding blocks, cork- or felt-backed, support abrasive paper while leveling the finish.

Rubbing oil, usually paraffin oil or mineral oil, lubricates polishing powders and steel wool as you rub out the finish.

Removing defects and smoothing

To remove defects and smooth a rough finish, start with 600-grit sandpaper. If the finish is very thin—for example, several coats of shellac or wiping varnish—use your hand to back the sandpaper. On thicker finishes you can use a backing block. Begin sanding with the grain. The finish should powder and not gum. If it gums, wait for the finish to dry longer. Wipe off the dust with a solvent-dampened cloth.

Bringing up the sheen

Gloss finishes require a two-step approach using a fine polishing compound to remove the 600-grit sanding scratches from the prior step. The second polishing compound is finer and breaks down into smaller particles as you use it, which is what eventually creates a glossy finish if you rub hard and long enough.

For satin finishes, use 0000 steel wool (or gray ultra-fine synthetic pads) to rub the surface after sanding with 600-grit sandpaper. The steel wool replaces the sandpaper scratches with much finer scratches.

First, rub with the grain using the steel wool dry (with no lubricant). This produces the low-luster finish that you'll find on very old furniture. Most people (myself included) like a higher luster. If that's the look you want, the final step is waxing. This step gives the wood more shine and an absolutely silky feel. The wax fills in the tiny hairline scratches left by the steel wool pad, resulting in a higher sheen. Use the same steel wool grade as before but with a wax–paint thinner mix. When the wax mix dries, buff the surface with a clean rag.

Wiping on a finish

Wiping varnishes are a great choice for first-time finishers. You don't need an expensive brush and the finish is less likely to develop bubbles or drips because it's applied thinly.

1. **Moisten an absorbent cotton cloth** with the wiping varnish or polyurethane. Pour the finish into the rag or paper towel right from the can.

2. **Wipe on the varnish** in smooth, even strokes. Overlap each stroke by about ½ in. Work with a light illuminating the back of the piece so you can see if you've missed a spot and correct it immediately. Clean up any drips or runs as you work.

3. **Use the corner or edge of the rag** to get the finish into corners or details. Once all surfaces are evenly coated with the finish, allow it to dry for 8 hours or longer.

4. **Sand lightly** with 320-grit sandpaper or a synthetic abrasive pad. Use a tack cloth to remove dust between coats. Apply as many coats as you wish, usually three to five, with light sanding in between.

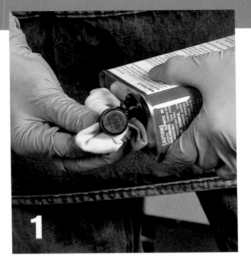

workSmart

Old cotton T-shirts are ideal for applying wiping finishes. You can also use a nontextured paper towel (like Viva®). After using the rags, lay them out flat to dry completely before disposing of them to avoid the risk of fire.

Brushing on a finish

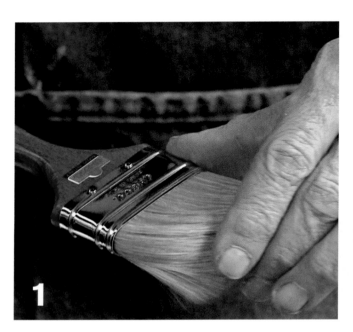

Make sure you use the correct brush for the finish you'll be using. Here, I'm using oil-based polyurethane, so I bought a good-quality 2-in. China-bristle brush at the store where I got the finish.

1. **Make sure the brush is clean** of dirt by flicking the bristles back and forth with your hand.

2. **Condition the brush** by dipping it up to the ferrule in the thinner for the finish you'll be using. Use water for water-based finishes, mineral spirits for oil-based varnishes, and alcohol for shellac.

3. **Strain the finish** into a smaller container through a medium-mesh strainer to remove any bits of debris or dried finish.

4. **Dip the brush into the finish halfway up** (never farther), and bring the brush out of the liquid. Press the brush against the side of the container to remove excess finish.

5. **Start in from an edge** and pull the brush to the outside.

6. **Overlap the previous stroke** by about half. When the brush runs out of finish, the bristles start to separate, causing streaks. Reload the brush and continue brushing and overlapping the strokes until you cover the surface.

Removing fisheye

If you see fisheyes, immediately wipe off your finishing product (oil-based stains will fisheye as well) before the finish starts to set up. Use the cleanup solvent for that particular finish.

1. **Wipe the surface with denatured alcohol** after the finish is removed. Allow the surface to dry.

2. **Scrub the surface well with TSP or a TSP substitute** and Scotch-Brite (green or maroon color). Mix the TSP with water according to the instructions on the product. Wipe the residue off with a clean cloth and allow the wood to dry. Smooth the grain if necessary with 220-grit sandpaper.

3. **Apply a coat of 2-lb. dewaxed shellac.** The alcohol base of shellac doesn't react to silicone the way that other finish solvents do, so the shellac isolates it and prevents the fisheye from reforming.

4. **When the shellac is dry,** you can apply any finish you wish over the shellac.

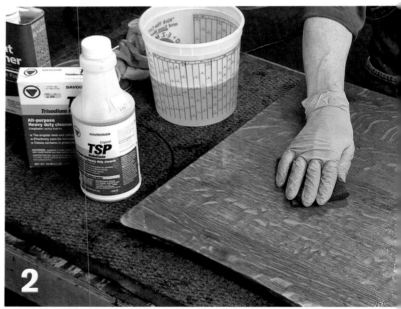

Rubbing a finish to gloss

Gloss finishes are a signature of high-style antique pieces. You can re-create a gloss finish using traditional materials to achieve that prized hand-rubbed look.

1. **Wrap a piece of 600-grit sandpaper around a block** and sand the surface with the grain until all the defects are gone and the finish feels smooth. If you use wet-or-dry sandpaper, use a lubricant.

2. **Wipe away the slurry with a rag** and then sprinkle some 4F pumice on the surface. Add some rubbing oil to make a paste and rub the surface several times. You can rub in any direction you wish.

3. **Remove the pumice–oil slurry with a clean rag** and then repeat Step 2, except substitute rottenstone for the 4F pumice. Make a paste with rubbing oil and rub several times.

4. **Wipe away some of the slurry to check your progress.** Add more rottenstone; oil if you need to and bear down harder as you progress. Stop when you get to the luster you're looking for.

workSmart

Between coats, you can use a sandpaper without a lubricant for water-based finishes. For oil-based finishes, use wet-or-dry paper with a lubricant.

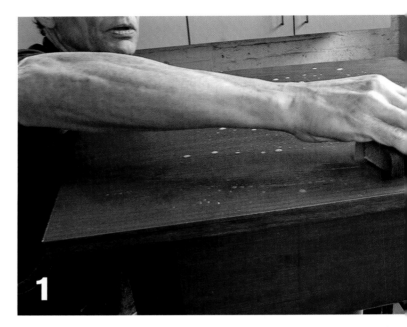

3

4

Power-rubbing a finish

Rubbing out with powders is a lot of work to do by hand. You can speed up the process (and save your arm) by using a power sander fitted with a polishing pad and polishing pastes.

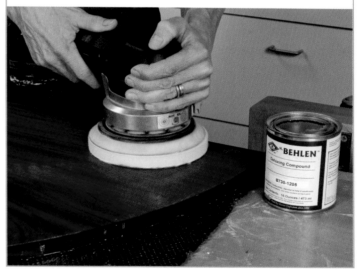

Rubbing a finish to satin

The procedure for rubbing to satin starts off the same as detailed in "Rubbing a finish to gloss" on p. 106, except that some of the materials and techniques change a bit. This process is what gives furniture a beautiful, silky surface that's as delightful to touch as it is to look at.

1. **Use 600-grit sandpaper** and a backing block to sand the surface level and remove the defects.

2. **Take a piece of 0000 steel wool,** unravel it, and then fold it back on itself to make a pad about the same size as the open palm of your hand.

3. **Rub in the direction of the grain,** using the steel wool dry (no lubricant). Most people have a tendency to avoid the edges, so rub the perimeter first, using short quick strokes. After you've finished the edges, you can use longer strokes to blend everything in. Always rub with the grain.

4. **For higher luster,** dip the pad into some paste wax and then pour a little paint thinner or mineral spirits on the pad. Use the same rub technique as described in Step 3.

5. **Polish off the excess wax** after it hazes (15 minutes to 20 minutes) with a microfiber or cotton cloth.

Minor repairs

No matter how well you care for furniture, ordinary use will result in dents, scratches, and other minor defects. A water glass, left to sit too long, softens finish, resulting in a white ring. The passage of time takes its toll on hardware too. Brass and other metals oxidize and discolor, leaving those once bright and shiny parts looking dull. Finishes themselves lose their luster over time.

Of course, you may want your piece to look really old. If you have to replace a hinge or some screws, you'll want it to blend with the older hardware. In this chapter, we look at those finishing touches that make a big difference as well as how to care for your furniture to keep it looking its best.

Both of these drawer pulls were cleaned, but the one on the left was rubbed with 0000 steel wool to highlight the high spots.

bath in lacquer thinner, scrub the hardware using brass-bristle brushes or steel wool. A lacquer thinner scrub with steel wool replicates the old look better than cleaning with polish.

After cleaning, highly polished brass will dull quickly unless it's shellacked or lacquered. Brass lacquer in aerosol spray cans is ideal for protecting brass, but it's not always easy to find. An alternative is aerosol shellac, which should be available at most paint and hardware stores.

Making new hardware look old

If you replace damaged hardware, especially hinges or screws, you may need to darken them so they match the older, original hardware. Chemical patination chemicals,

Hardware

Cleaning or repolishing metal hardware adds to the improved look of your refinishing project. You can just use steel wool and polishes to make it look brand new or slightly new. And if you must replace hardware, you can "age" it so that it matches existing hardware better.

Cleaning hardware

Metal hardware can be cleaned and brightened by soaking it in lacquer thinner or applying metal polish. After a

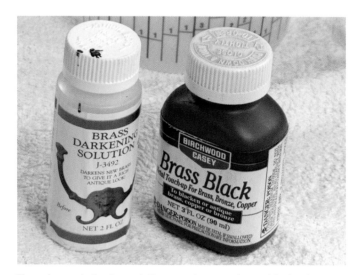

These brass-darkening solutions are inexpensive and had to be mail-ordered, but they both worked as advertised.

Brass screws and hinges are the likely parts that need to be replaced on old furniture.

also called brass-darkening solutions (see the bottom photo on p. 111), are relatively easy to find and will darken most metals.

Soak the hardware in the solution or apply it with a swab. When the metal turns the desired color, rinse it with water to stop the darkening processes. This process is particularly handy for old brass screws and hinges, which seem to get the most damage and need to be replaced.

You can also darken brass with household ammonia vapors. It's a lot slower than the chemical patination products, but one distinct advantage is that because it's slower you can really dial in the level of darkening you want.

Remove all the lacquer first

When darkening hardware, make certain to remove all the lacquer first. Any residual lacquer will resist the chemical resulting in an uneven effect.

Fixing minor surface damage

Most surface problems are easy to repair, especially once you've finished a piece and understand the process. Here are the solutions to some of the more common problems.

Stickers and tape (masking or clear) can leave a residue. Naphtha works best to remove it because it won't harm any finish. If the residue is really old, put a

To remove tape and old sticker residue, use naphtha.

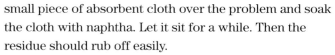
For crayon marks, use naphtha. For magic markers, use rubbing alcohol if naphtha doesn't work.

White marks in clear finishes can be caused by moisture or heat.

small piece of absorbent cloth over the problem and soak the cloth with naphtha. Let it sit for a while. Then the residue should rub off easily.

Crayon marks and felt-tip marker stains will usually come off after rubbing with naphtha. If not, a little rubbing alcohol (isopropyl alcohol) works. But don't let it sit on the surface too long or it may mar it.

Scrapes where the finish and stain are missing can be covered with colored furniture markers available at hardware and home centers. You can also use a matching stain and apply it with a small brush.

Scratches can be disguised with a product called "scratch cover" or you can try solvent reviver (see Chapter 4). If the scratches are deep enough that you can feel them with your fingernail, you can also rub them out with fine sandpaper.

White marks from a wet glass or hot items may disappear on their own after several days. If not, a light rubbing with mineral oil and rottenstone polishing powder will usually do the trick. Otherwise, try rubbing the area in a pendulum motion with a soft cloth moistened with a little denatured alcohol.

Furniture markers in a variety of wood-tone colors are available at home centers and paint stores. They make it easy to disguise scrapes and scratches.

Wax repair sticks are an easy way to fill small dents and gouges and are sold in wood-tone colors.

Paste wax is a classic way to take care of older furniture with lacquer or shellac finishes.

Black rings are underneath the finish and in the wood. This defect can be remedied only by removing the finish and bleaching the black stains with oxalic acid (see "Using oxalic acid wood bleach" on p. 75).

Small dents and gouges can be filled with wax repair sticks. The sticks are sold in sets or in individual colors. Rub the wax into the depression and then wipe off the excess.

General care of finishes

For bringing up the shine on antiques and old furniture finished with lacquer and shellac, nothing beats a good paste wax. Clean the surface first with naphtha. Then put some wax in the center of a cloth to make a wax applicator ball. Apply the wax thinly and evenly. Let it dry just a bit until it dulls (hazes). Then buff the surface vigorously with a clean cloth.

For modern finishes like varnish, polyurethane, and water-based finishes, clean first with water and a little bit of dishwashing detergent—around a capful of detergent to a cup of water. Apply the cleaning solution with a rag. Then wipe the finish clean with a soft, dry cloth. This will remove almost all residue from food, dirty hands, and other sources of grimy buildup. If you like a bit a luster, use a commercial furniture polish. Just don't overdo it. A little goes a long way.

Cleaning and polishing brass hardware

This brass hardware was so dark you couldn't even tell it was brass. More than likely it was much brighter when it was new.

1. **Start with clean, unfinished metal.** To remove old finishes that may have been on the metal, soak the hardware in furniture stripper overnight.

2. **Brush off the residue** of old finishes with a soft-bristle brush or 00 steel wool. Then rinse it in lacquer thinner.

3. **Use a soft, brass-bristle brush** to scrub the surface. The hardware will be clean but may still be quite dark and dull after this step. You can stop here if you want to preserve the old look.

4. **For more shine** and to emphasize the highlight, rub the hardware with 0000 steel wool.

5. **To polish the brass to a high shine,** use a commercial brass or metal polish.

warning

When cleaning hardware with furniture stripper, always use heavy, chemical-resistant gloves and protect your eyes with safety glasses.

Antiquing metal hardware

Sometimes you may want to replace or update the hardware on your project, or you may be missing a part like a hinge and just need to darken it so it looks old. This is easily done with a chemical sold specifically for darkening brass, copper, and bronze. Most new hardware is lacquered so it stays shiny. You'll have to remove the lacquer for the chemical to work.

1. **Pour some lacquer thinner** in a container with a lid and let the brass parts soak overnight. Remove the hardware.

2. **Use 0000 steel wool** to remove all the lacquer from the brass.

3. **Dry off the brass** and then place the hardware in the darkening solution. You can remove it when it looks dark enough. If you want to stop further darkening, rinse it immediately under water.

4. **A darkened hinge** looks more authentically old than a new one.

Darkening brass with ammonia

The darkening solutions can be hard to find locally. This procedure using common household ammonia also works; it just takes longer. I needed to replace some brass screws I stripped when I removed them from the coat tree. Screws aren't lacquered so I don't need to strip off any lacquer. However if you have hinges or hardware to darken, they probably have lacquer so it would be best to soak them in lacquer thinner first as described in "Antiquing metal hardware" on the facing page.

1. **Assemble your supplies.** You'll need a small container to hold your parts, a larger container with a tight-sealing lid to put the small one inside, and some household ammonia. Buy fresh ammonia.

2. **Put about 1 oz. ammonia in the large container.** Place the parts you want to darken in the small container (with no ammonia) and place it inside the larger one. (Don't let the brass parts touch the liquid ammonia. It's the ammonia vapor that does the darkening.) Tightly seal the large container.

3. **Check the progress of the effect after a few hours.** When the hardware has reached the desired level of darkening, rinse the parts under cold water to prevent further darkening.

Waxing furniture

Waxing used to be the preferred method of caring for furniture, but modern finishes, such as polyurethane and water-based products, don't respond well to waxing. If the finish on your project is shellac, wiping varnish, or solvent lacquer or if you have an antique that just needs to be spruced up, consider waxing it.

1. **Put a scoop of paste wax** inside an open cloth.

2. **Fold the cloth over on itself** to make a paste wax applicator ball. Squeeze until you see some wax coming out.

3. **Apply the wax thinly** over the wood.

4. **When the wax hazes** after 15 minutes or so, buff the surface to a shine with a clean cloth.

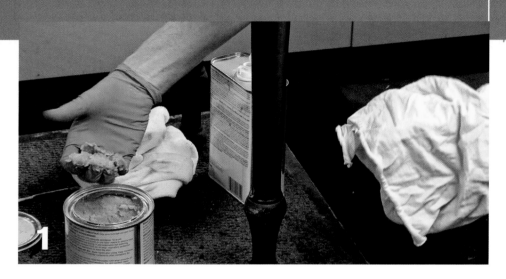

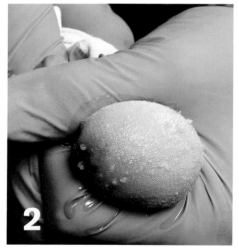

Cleaning furniture

Modern furniture finishes like polyurethane, varnishes, and water-based finishes are best cleaned on a regular basis. You can spend hundreds of dollars on gimmicky cleaners, but here is the method I use on my own furniture.

1. **Put 1 oz. of Dawn dishwashing detergent in a plant mister bottle.** Fill the bottle up to the top with water (usually about 16 oz.).

2. **Spritz the soapy water on the furniture.** Then take a clean rag and wipe the surface clean. The soapy water removes both oil- and water-soluble grime.

3. **For a higher luster**, use one of the popular lemon-oil products, such as Pledge® or a furniture two-in-one cleaner and polish like the one I'm using here.

resources

You should be able to find most of the supplies mentioned in this book at most local hardware stores, paint stores, or home centers. For supplies not available in your local area, check these online sources.

Furniture stripping and refinishing supplies

- **Constantine's Wood Center**
  (800) 443-9667
  www.constantines.com

- **Homestead Finishing Products**
  (866) 631-5429
  www.homesteadfinishingproducts.com

- **Finishing Products**®
  (800) 229-0934
  www.hoodfinishing.com

- **Klingspor**® **Woodworking Shop**
  (800) 228-0000
  www.woodworkingshop.com

- **Woodcraft**®
  (800) 535-4486
  www.woodcraft.com

- **Woodworker's Supply, Inc.**®
  (800) 645-9292
  www.woodworker.com

Hardware

- **Lee Valley Tools**®
  From US: (800) 871-8158
  From Canada: (800) 267-8767
  www.leevalley.com

- **Rockler**® **Woodworking and Hardware**
  (800) 279-4441
  www.rockler.com

- **Van Dyke's Restorers**®
  (800)-558-1234
  www.vandykes.com

index